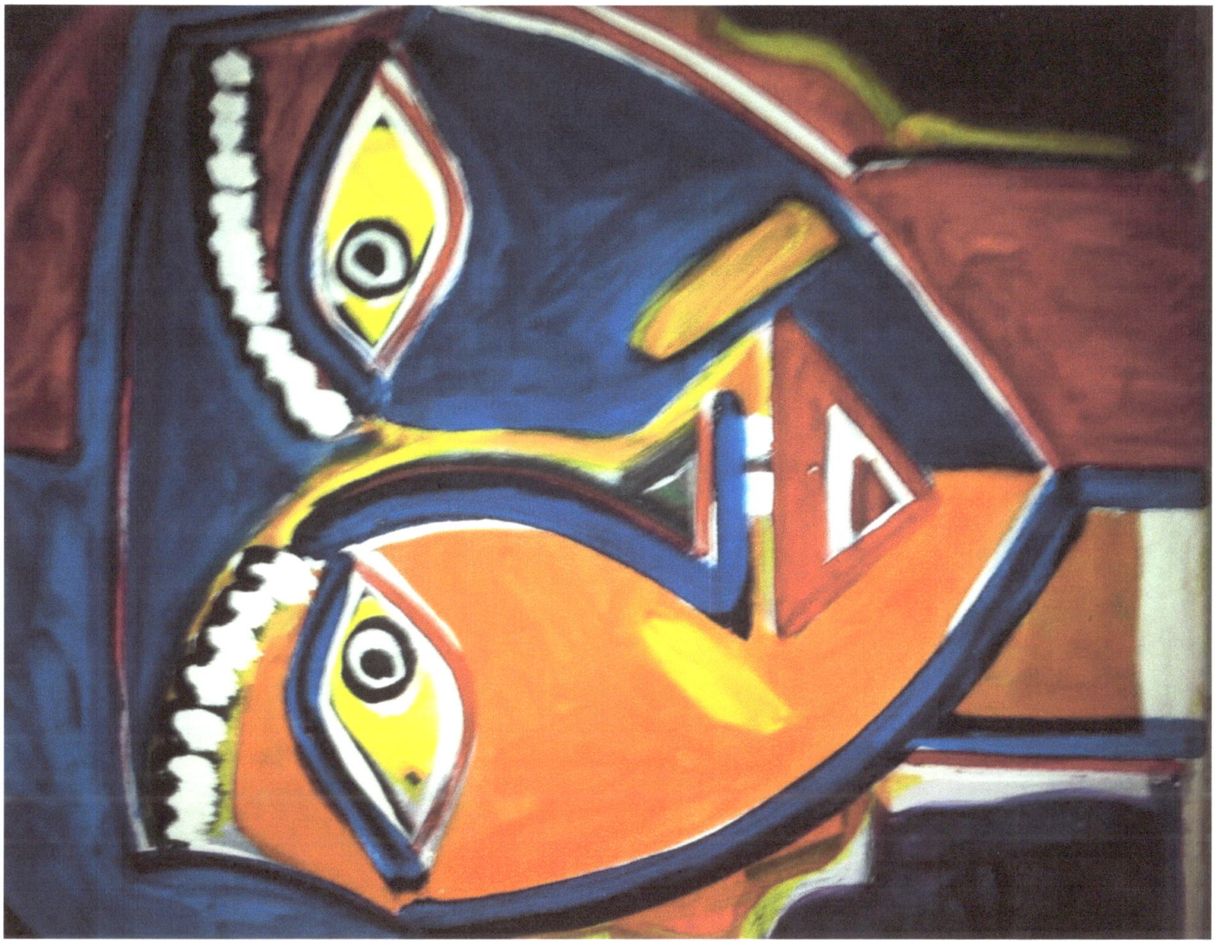

At first, I start with alien human as I worry about my bone and chemistry accident. It is possible with my imagine. So I love today to live as God's beautiful body as an idol.

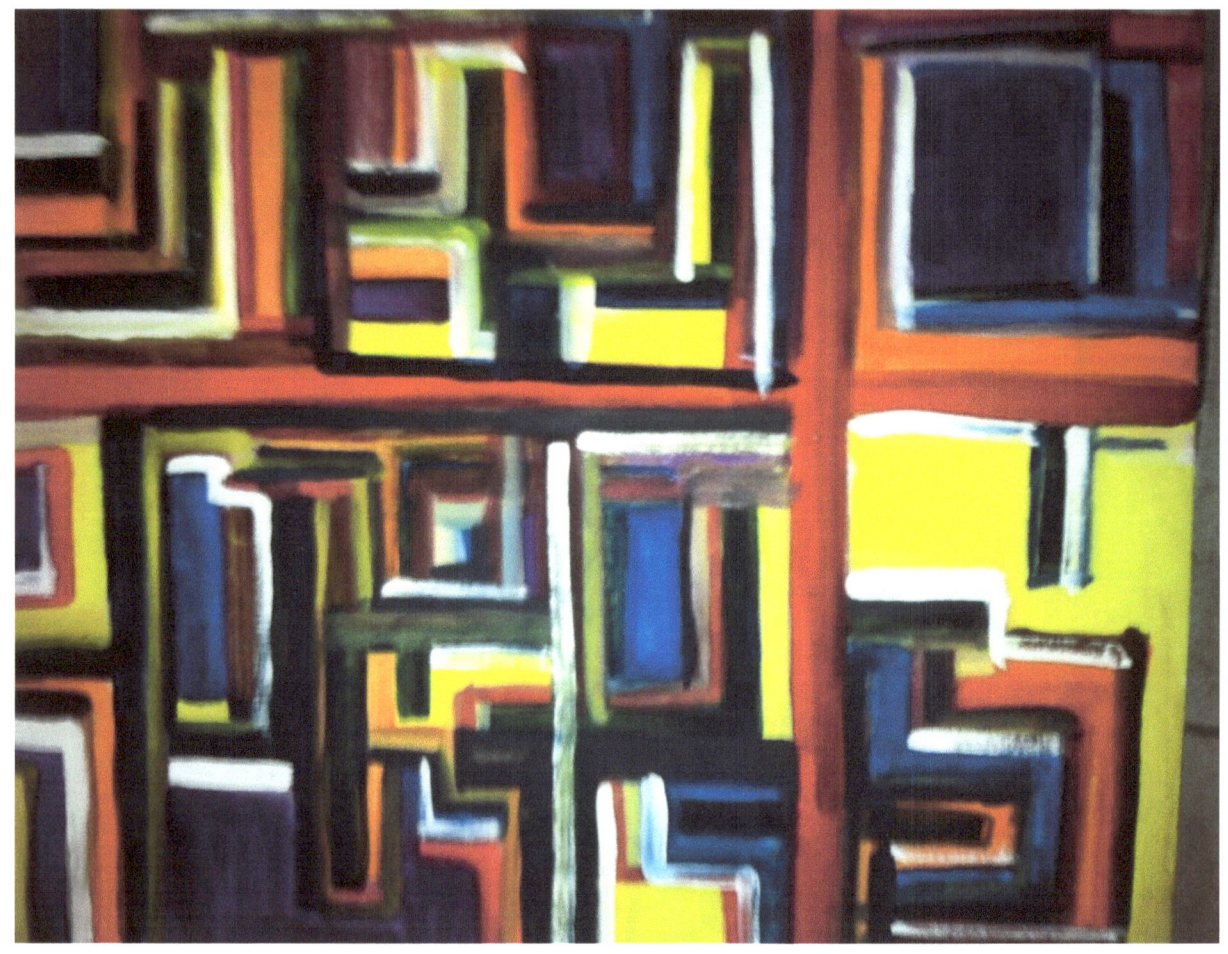

There are a lot of hidden way in my brain to dizzy and tired of phobia, so I love to sleep in my dark black room.

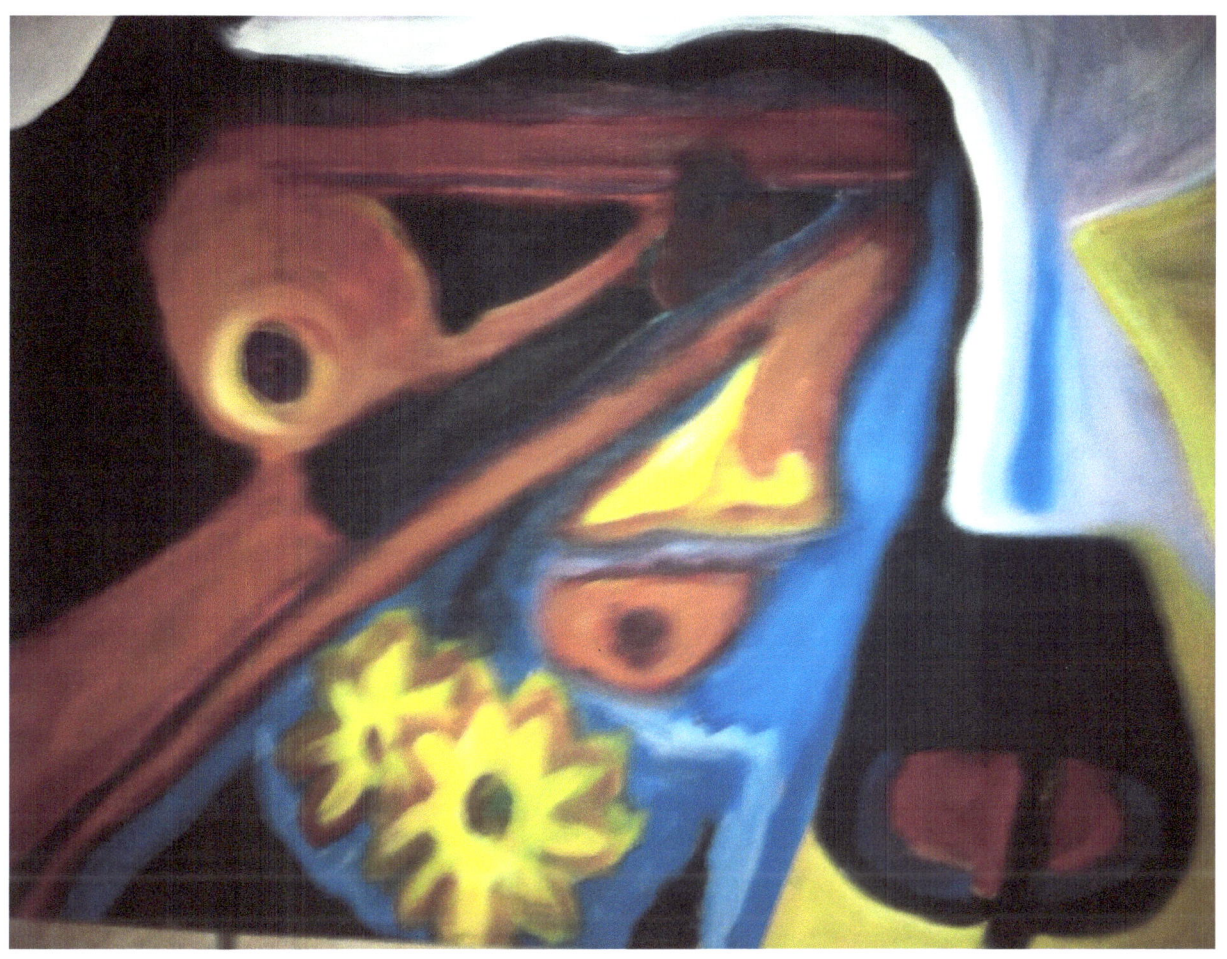

And when I get comfortable after the nightmare, I think how it would be to live in the soft farm.

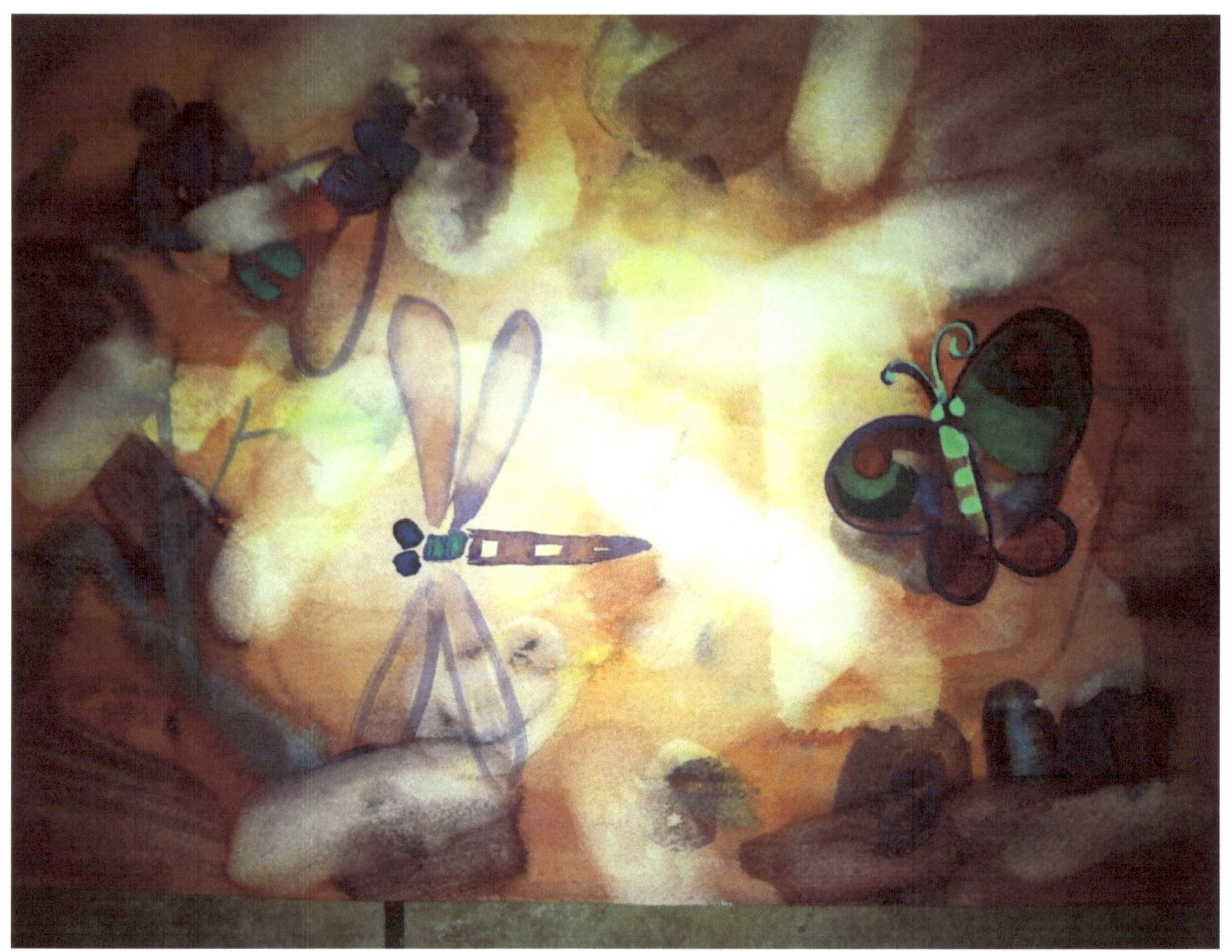

So I do the labor to live in the country as the farmer. The result is that there were no love for me as I can be the alien, and I misunderstand to be the butterfly wing on my back shoulder as alien by chemical.

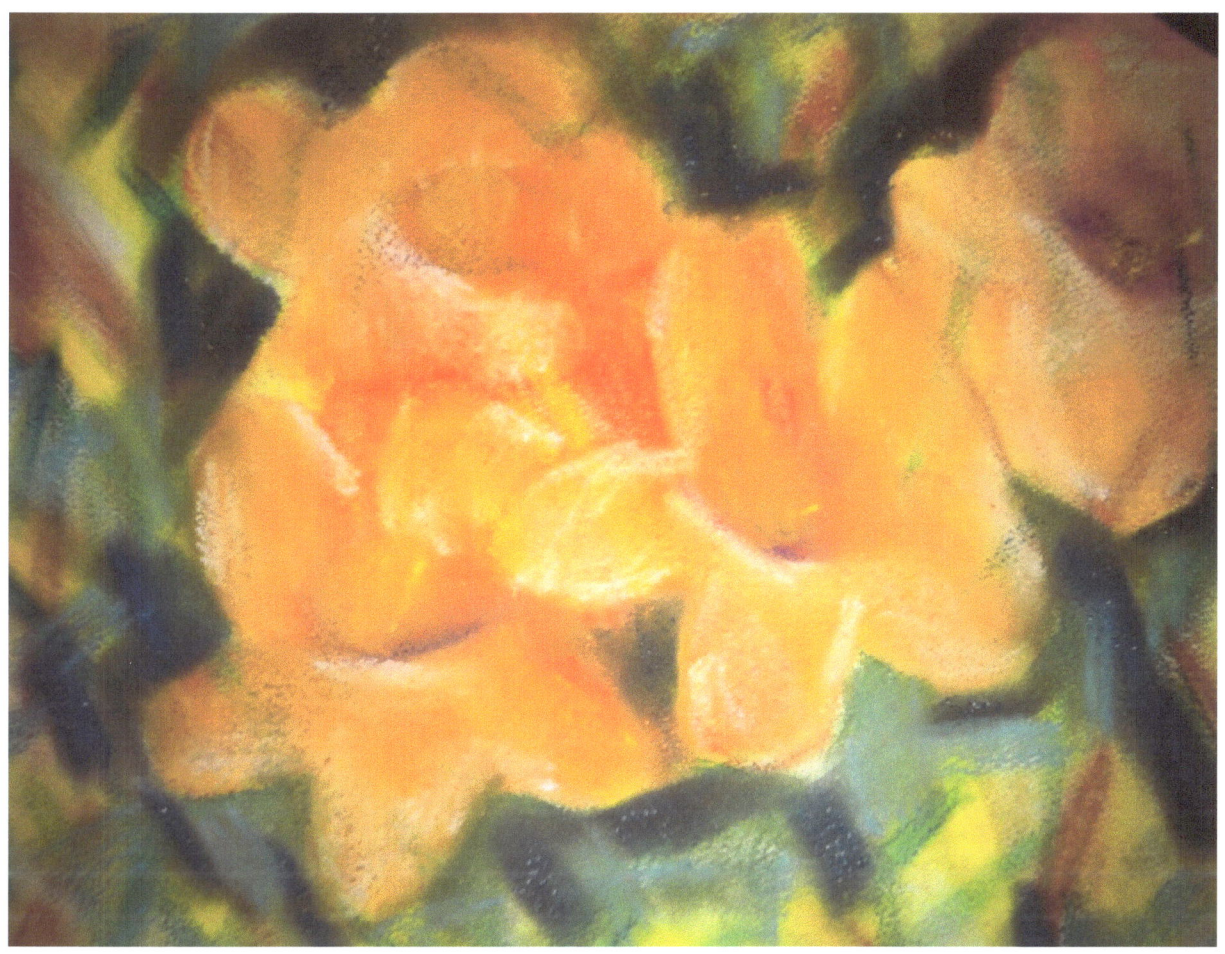

Still I know that I am the human and I can go to the
heaven to be the truth of the world. But it also makes me
to be monster again as the smooth chemical thief.

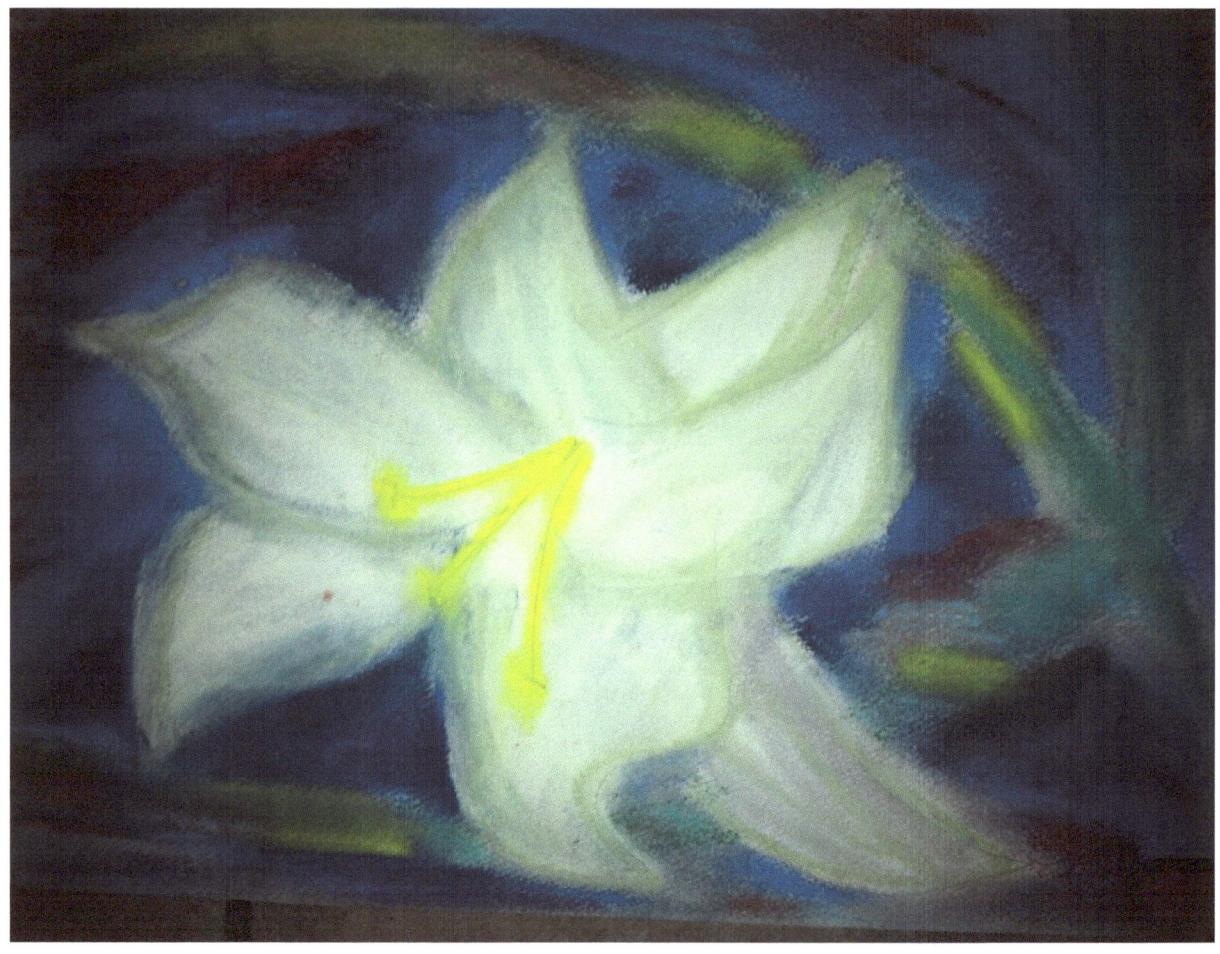

But fortunately, the flower does not have the eyes, ears and nose, so it is also the alien without my human. And I fly the sky as free on the flower life. It is the imagine picture to love in the alien world as no earth to stand up.

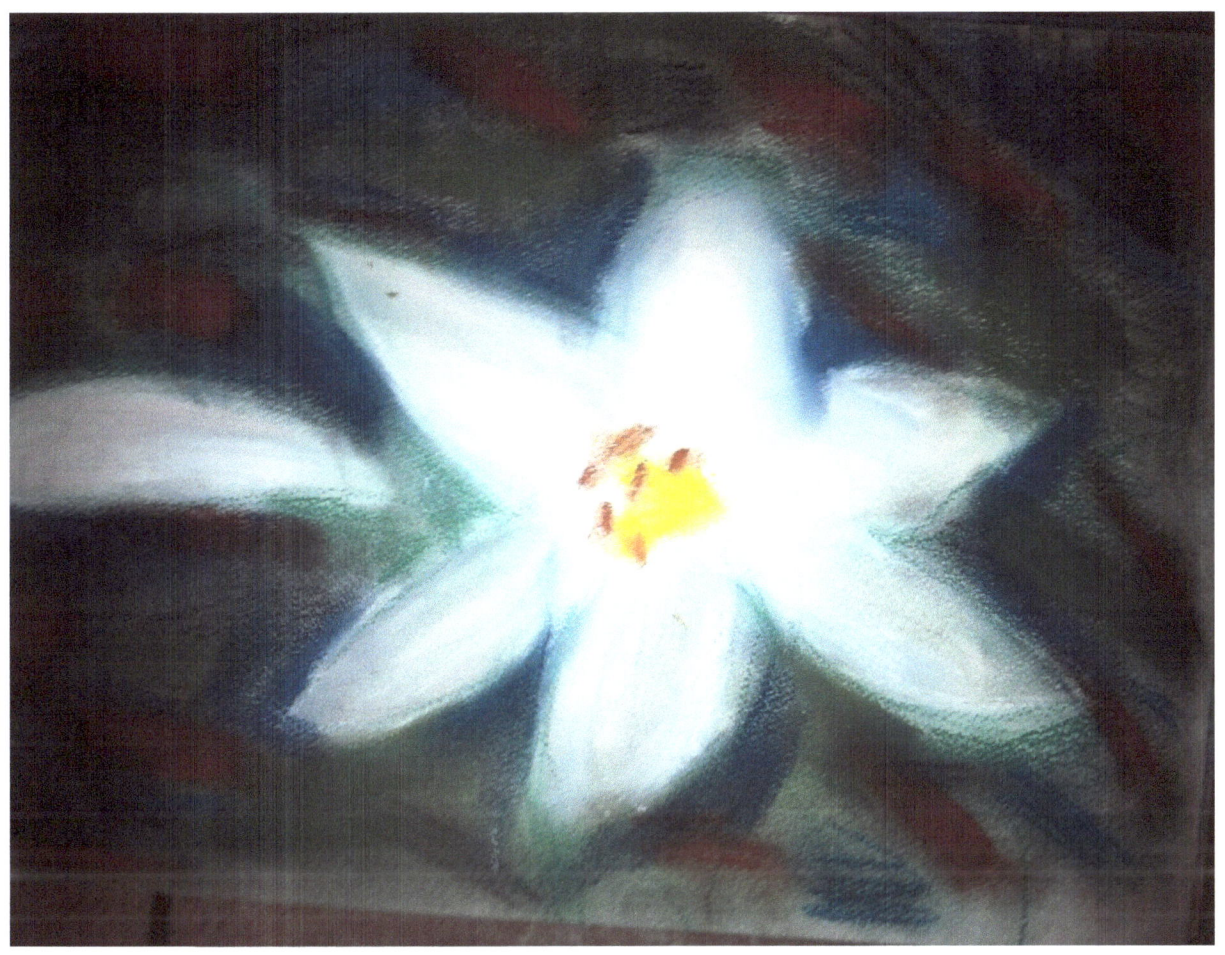

The green color is the basic color for the alien flower, and
I sleep on the nowhere in the space as the flower to be
another kind of existence.

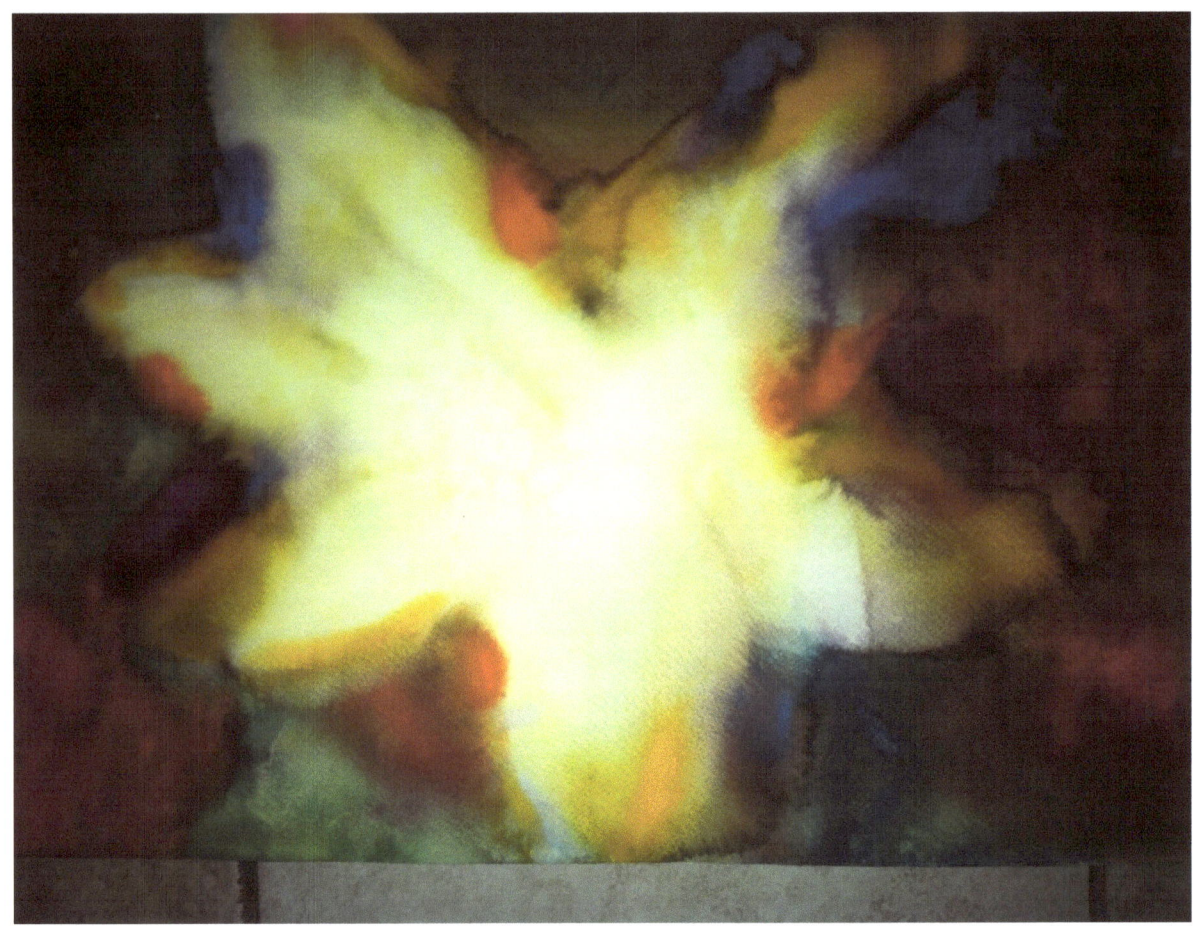

Suddenly, the sky light the thunder and the flower of my body blooded as the dust away to the feeling of the letter to send to my girl.

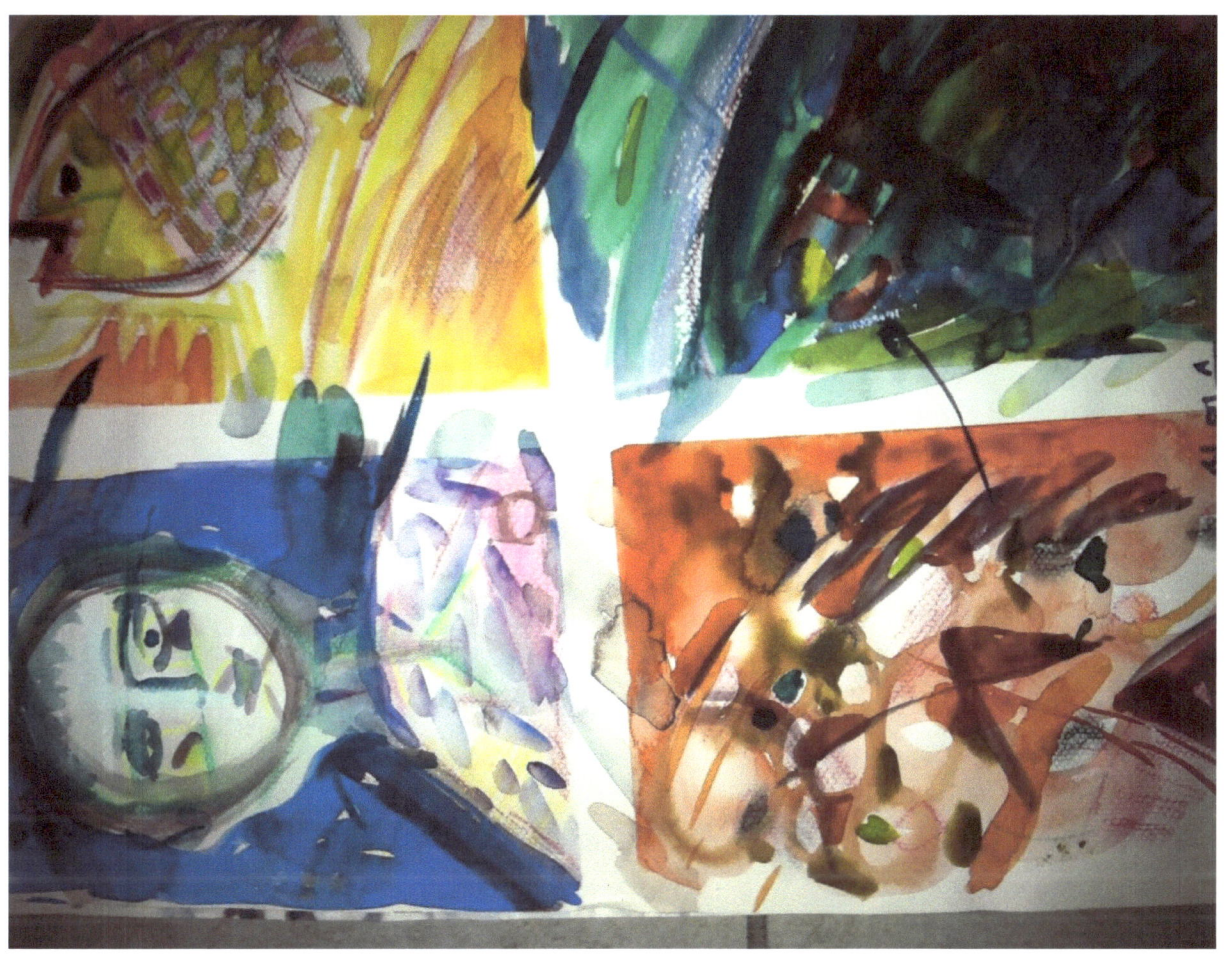

Still I remember my face a long time ago as the real man's body. It was divided into my art picture and fade away into another world to love to the heaven.

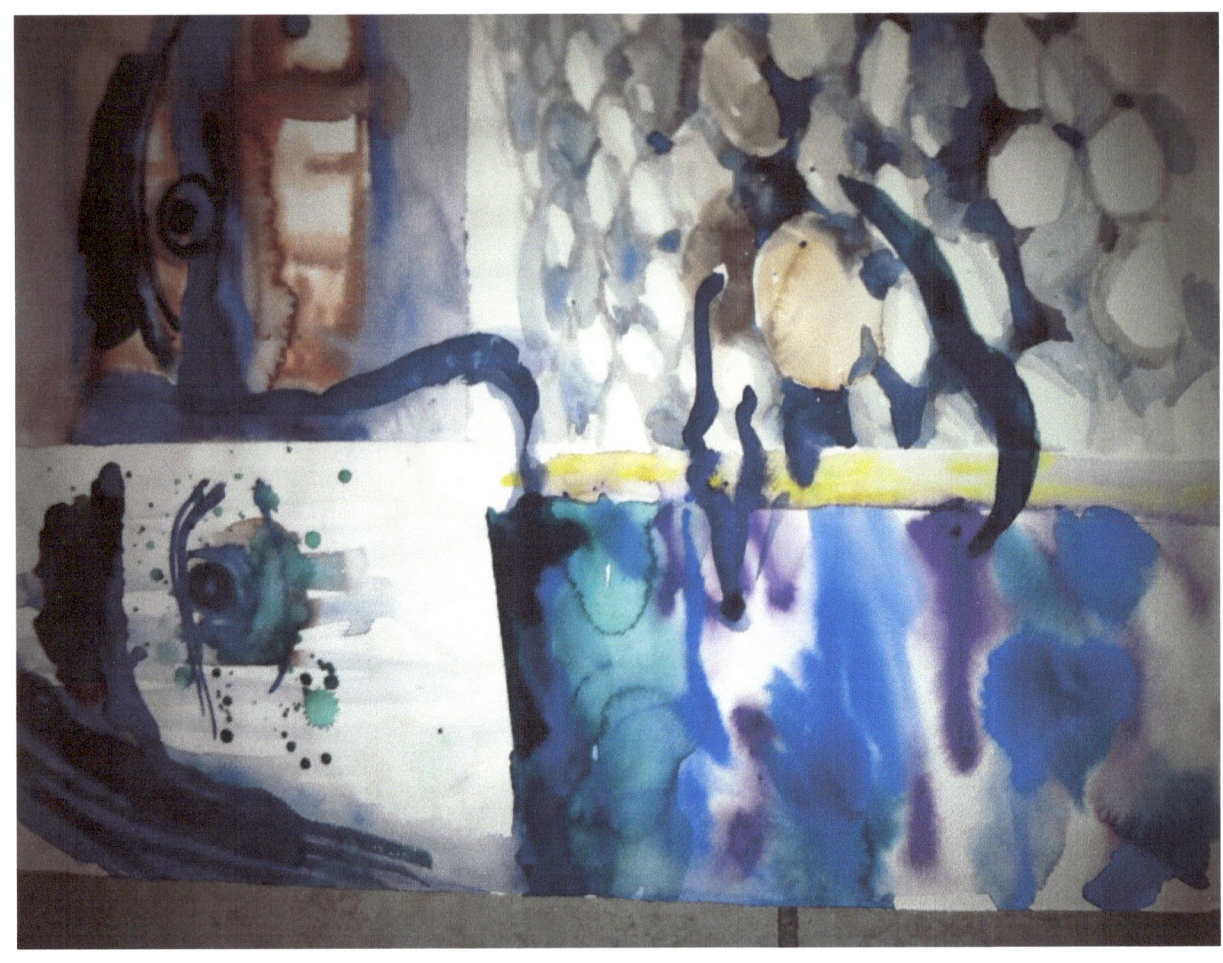

And it becomes Jesus as the blue love for my new love, so I cannot love you with the pain. Jesus is in the blue for the new age as satan and evil.

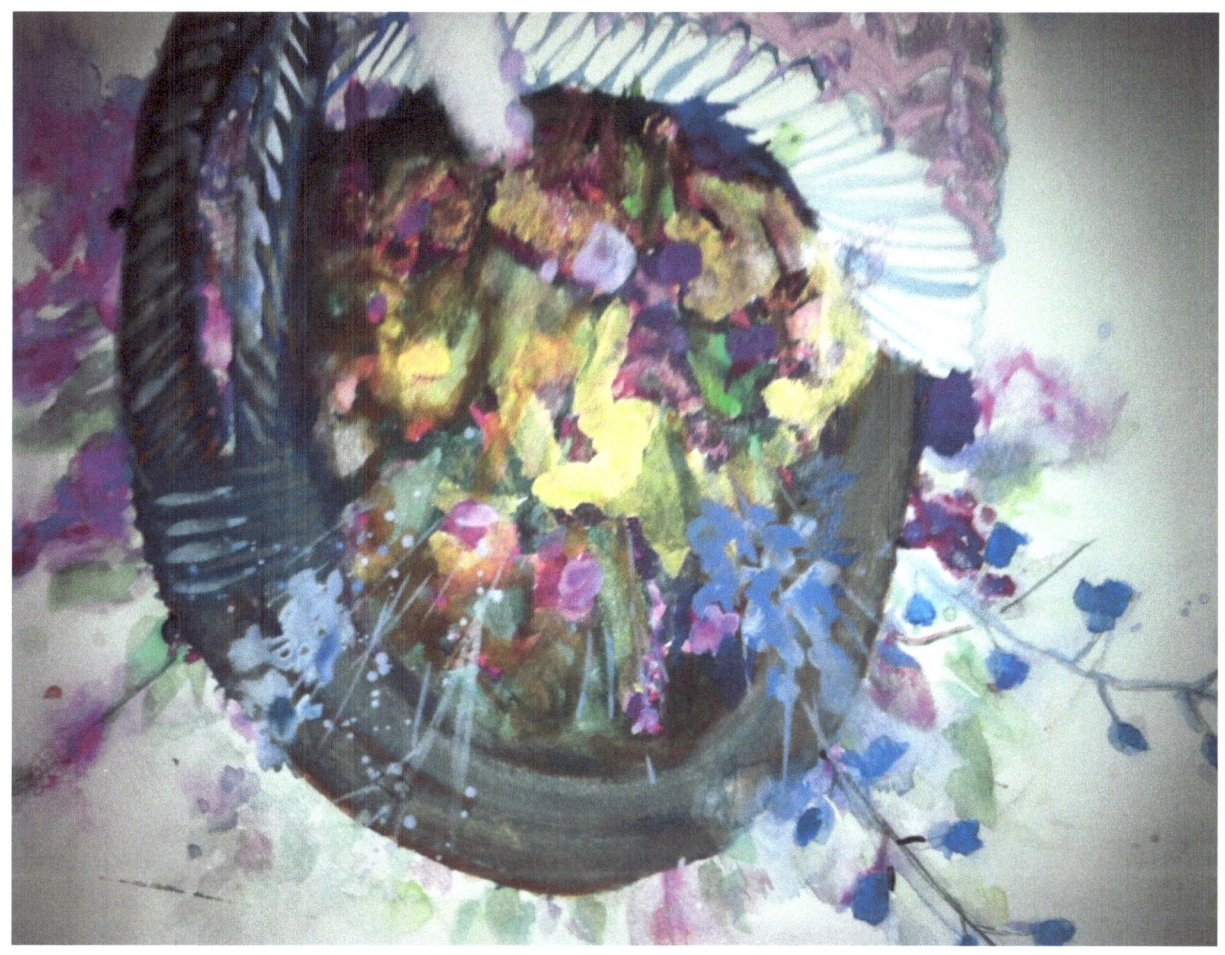

Sometimes it looks like the beautiful picture, and the best love for you all over the world. And the flower kills me again so I become the alien to be the monster.

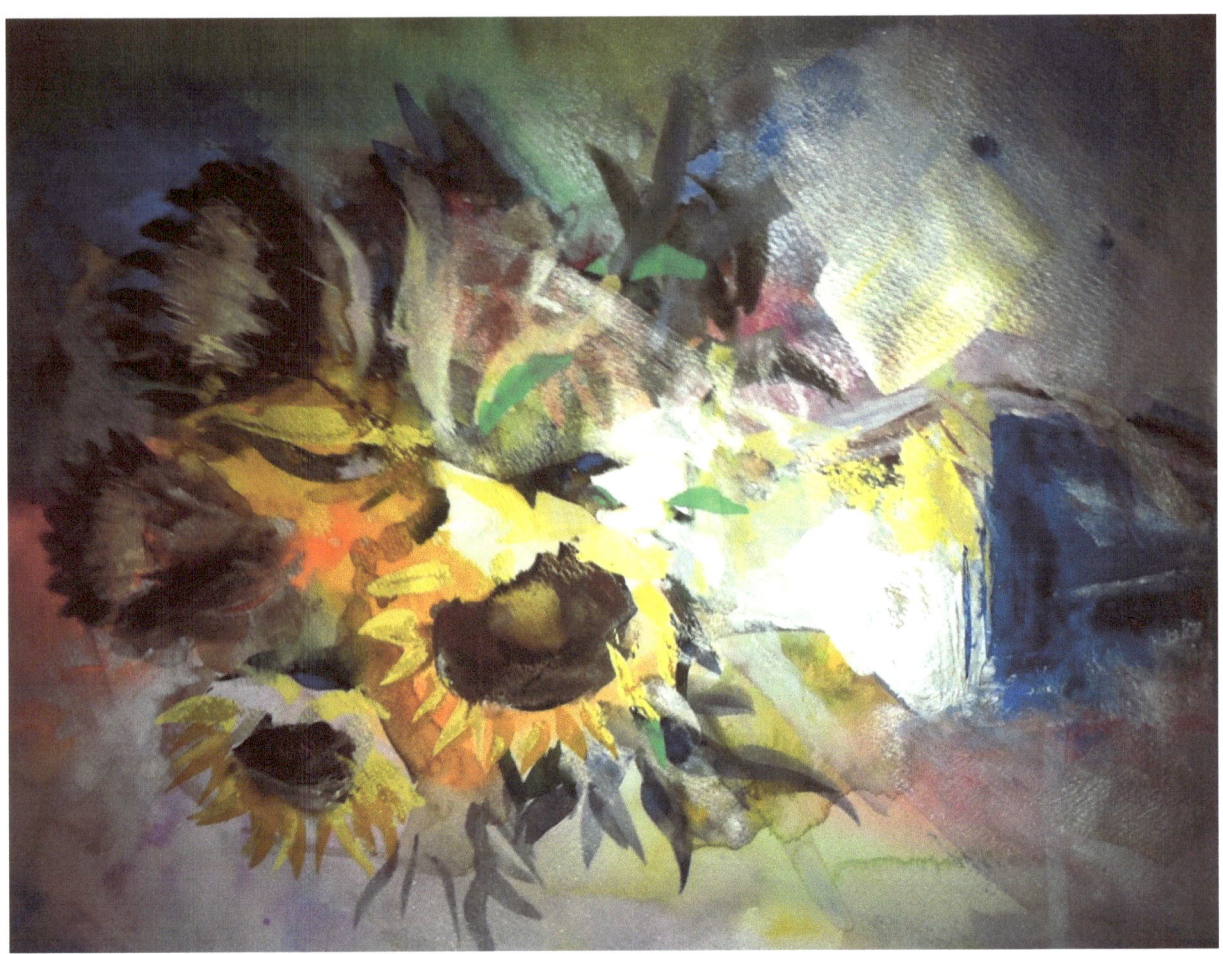

Just like Van gogh, I feel sunflower is the best theme to write my poem as the poem is the sunflower. I go through with my picture into the sky to be monster or the butterfly or the great prince. This feeling is with me to love the girl for my sunflower as forever.

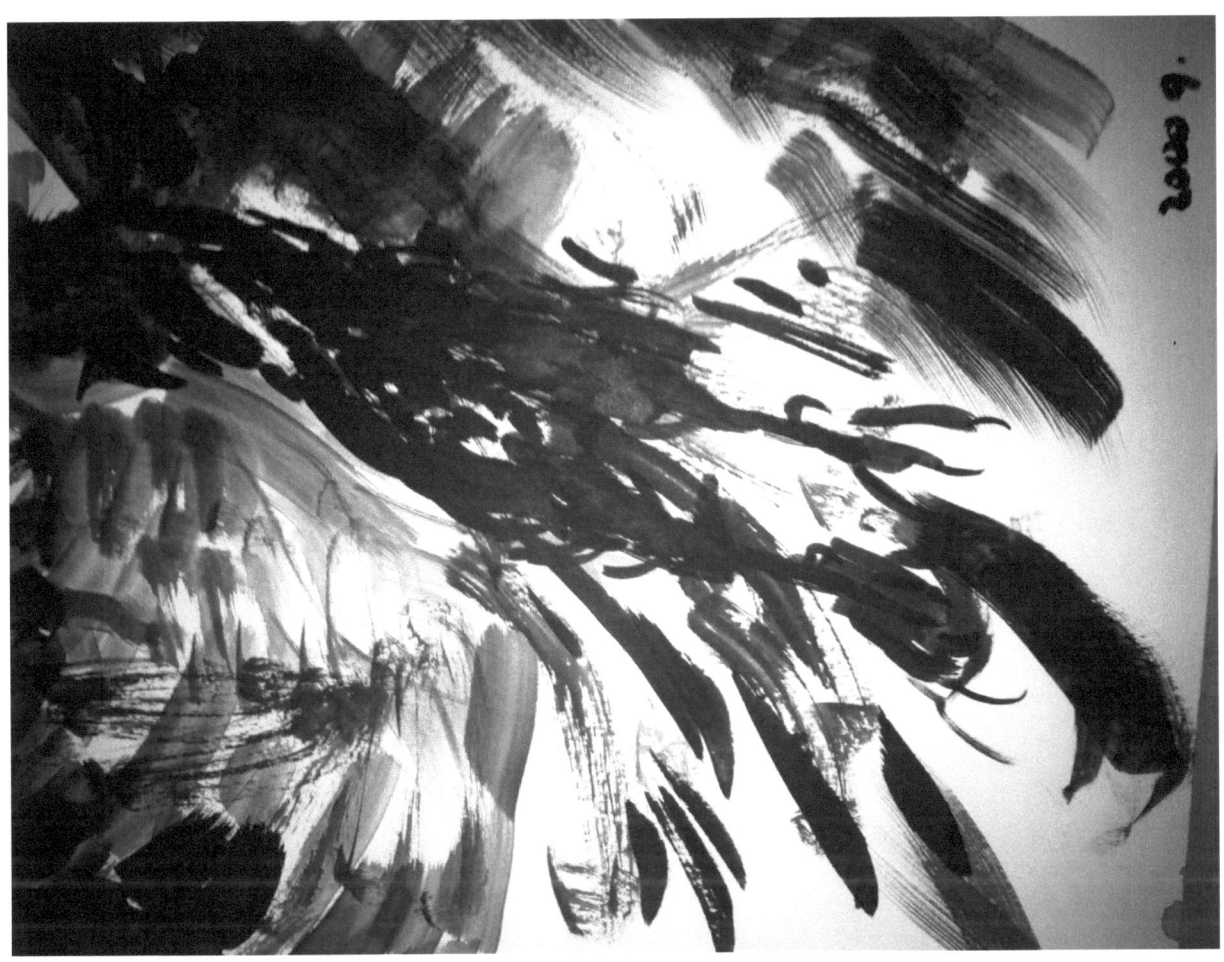

Sometimes the black line is so powerful and strong to hug the woman. So I just let it fly away as I can move and exercise my body as the practice my mind.

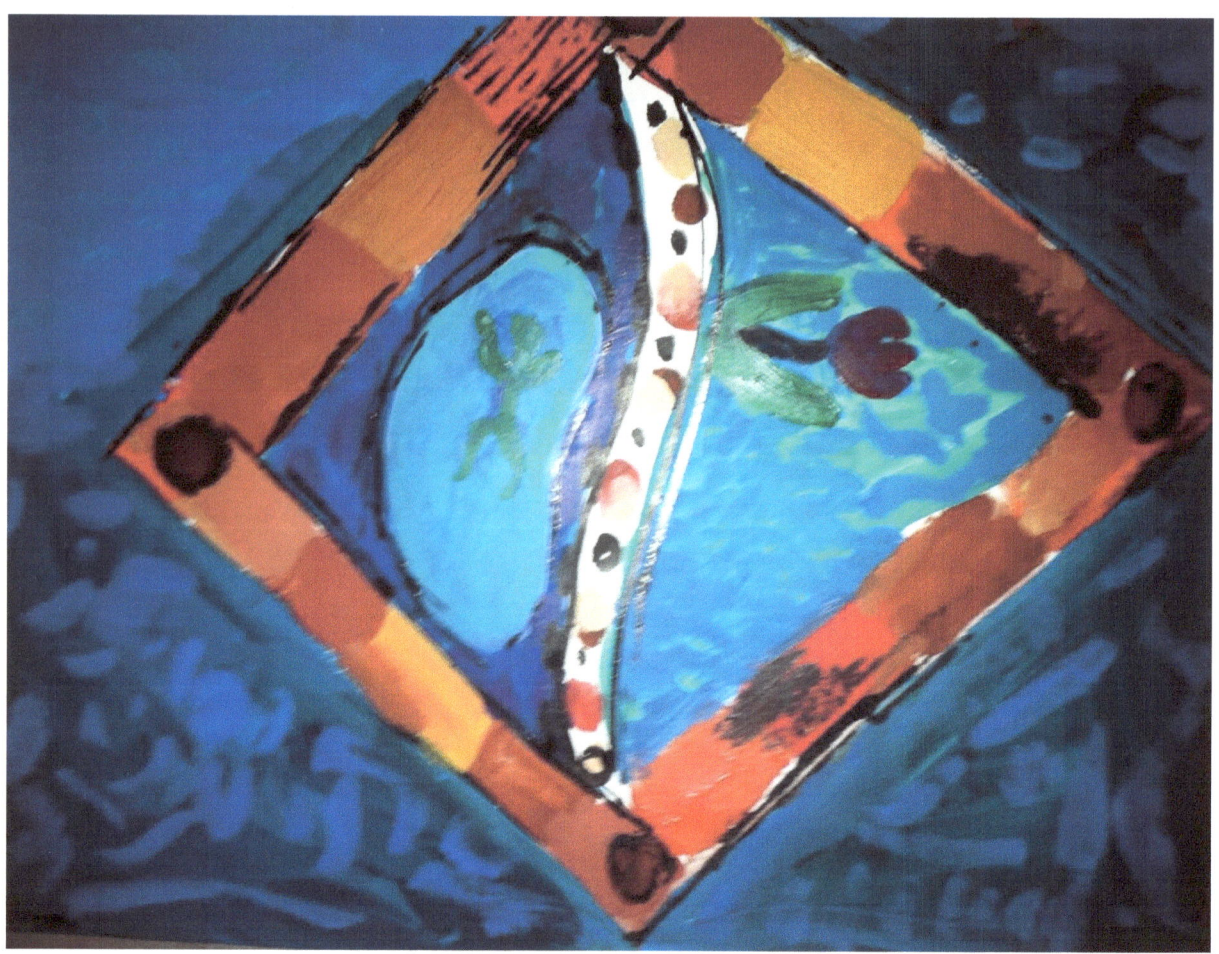

The square is upside stand up to be comfortable and calmful. So I draw the little flower inside it so my lover is sleeping another side of flower with the border line.

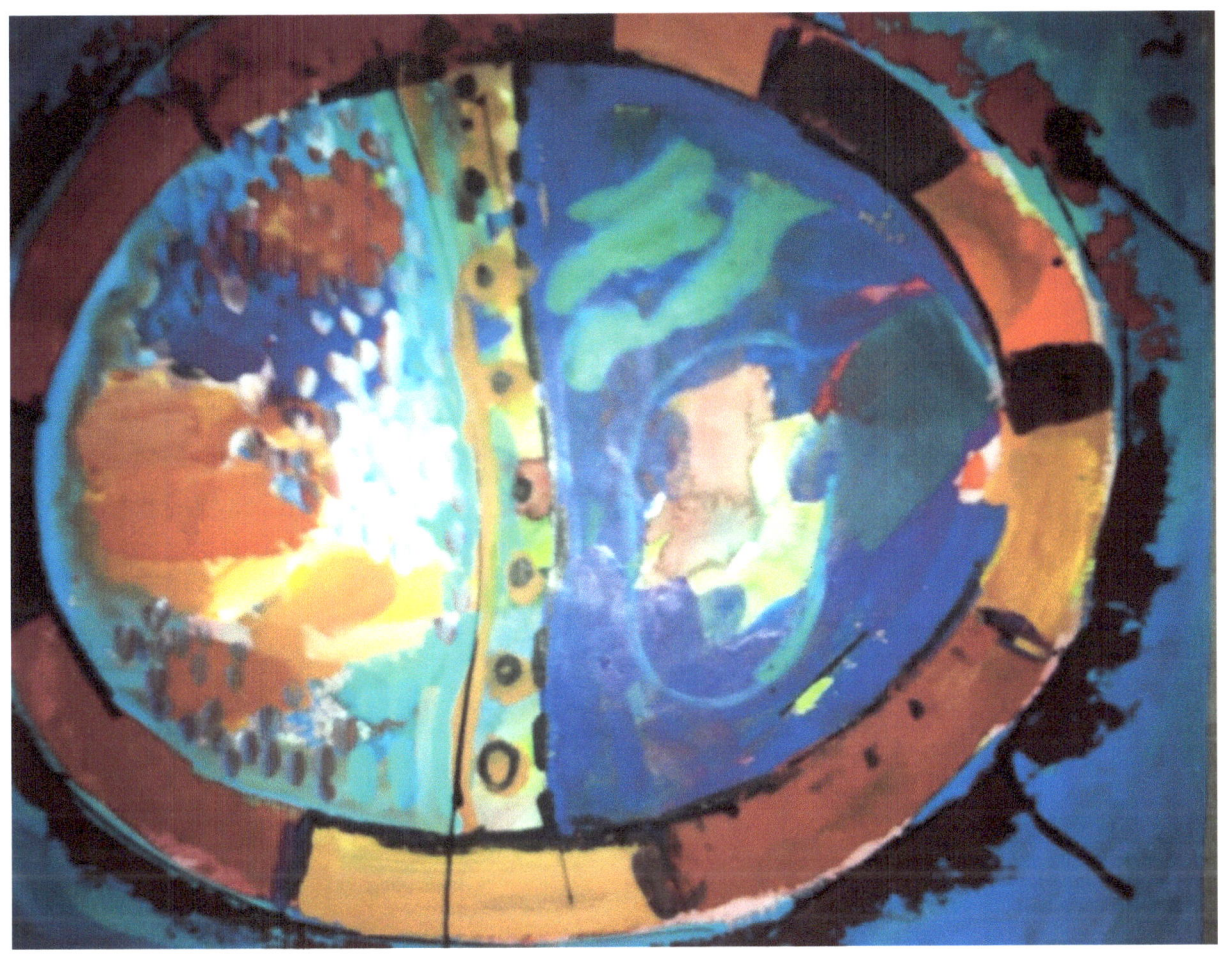

And it made another kind of creature and mixed together as the big bang of the world. And the new world is beginning here for my love.

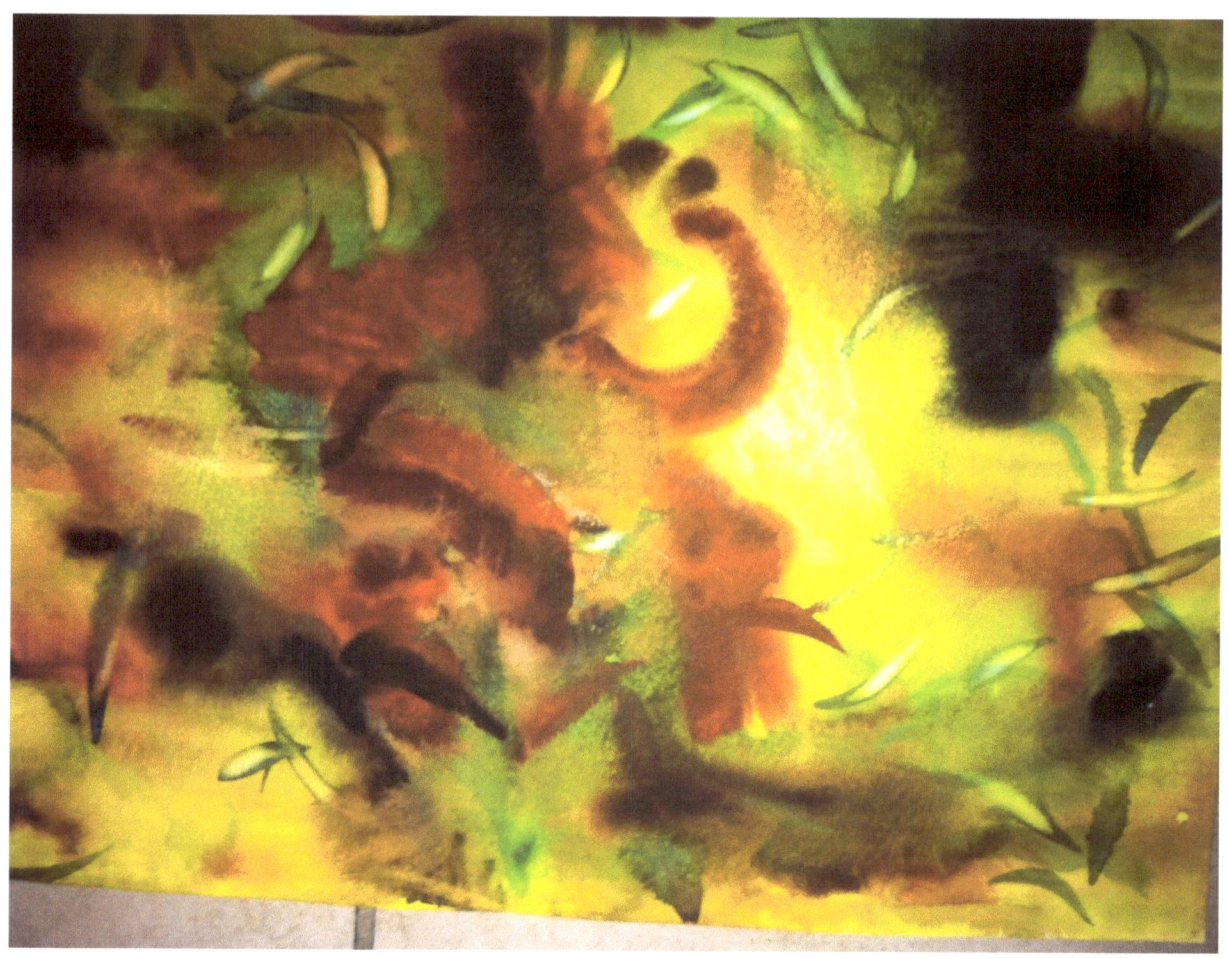

The flower is dust away as the dust so it is burn out. And the world is new beginning of the red sunset to my new love. It is soft to love in the sky with the dust of the flower.

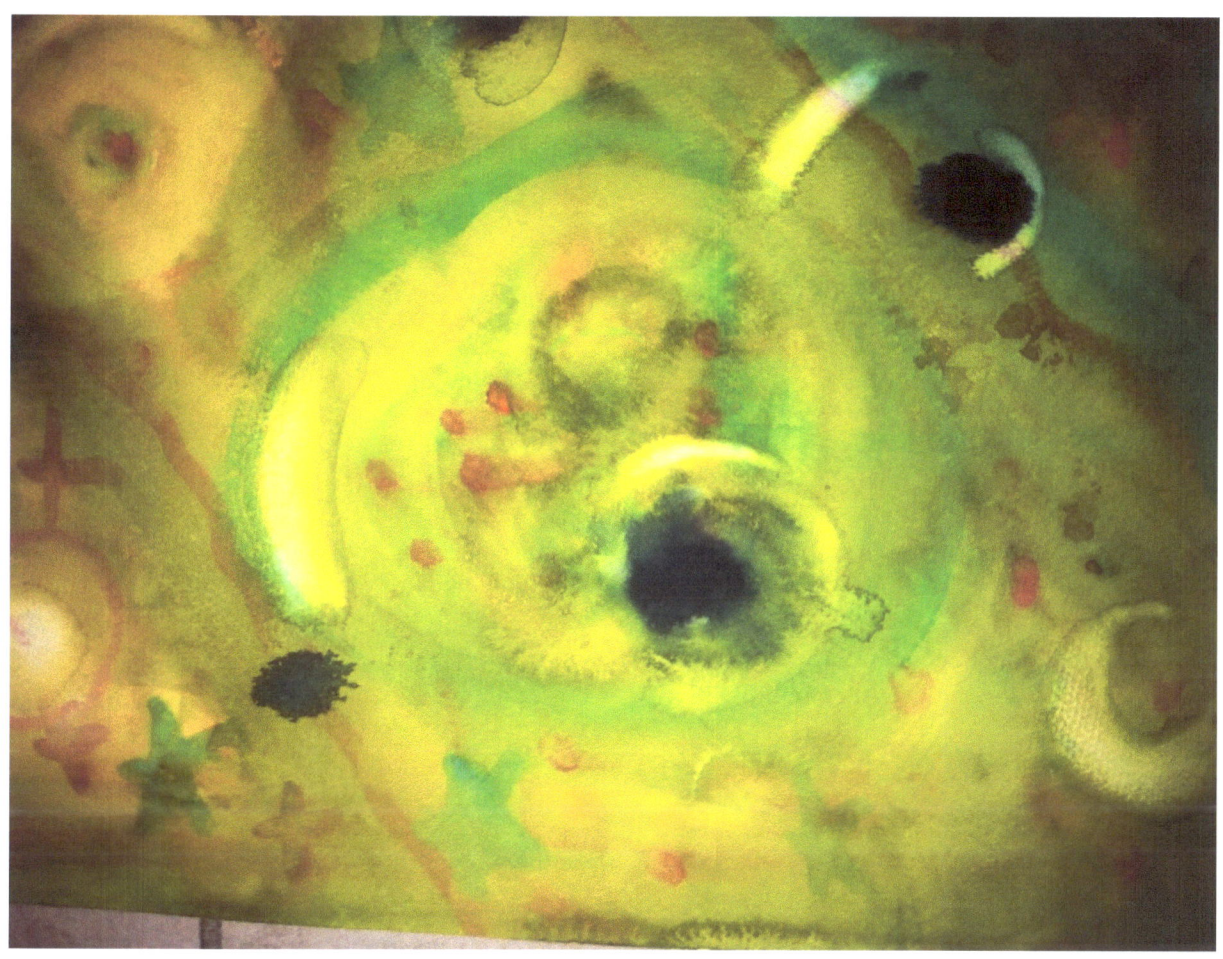

And the dead flower again mixed together to make another world. It is the death baby to remember my lover for himself lonely but happy himself.

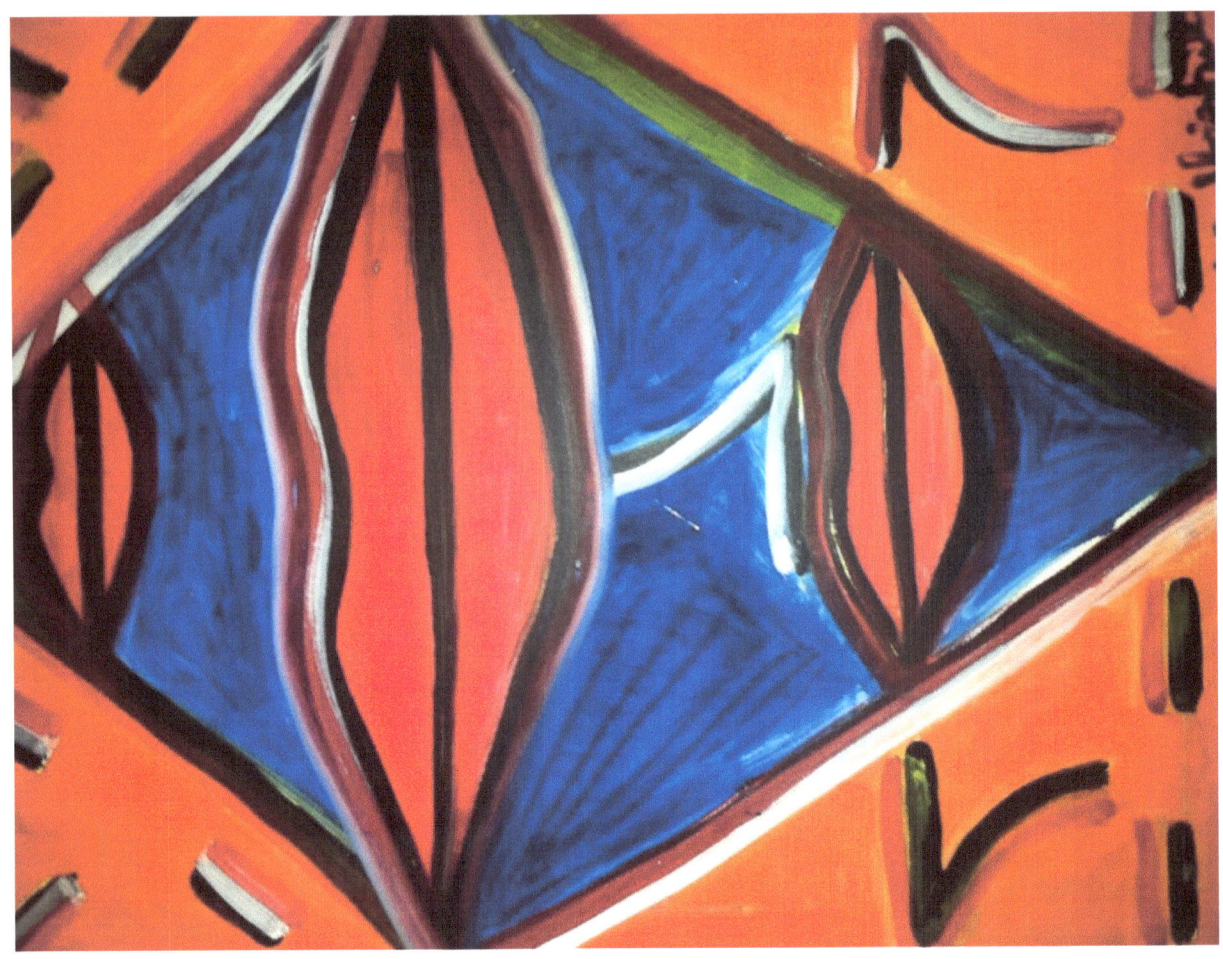

And suddenly the new thing happened as the lip of the woman. It is called the kiss but it is the good feeling to love the honest world.

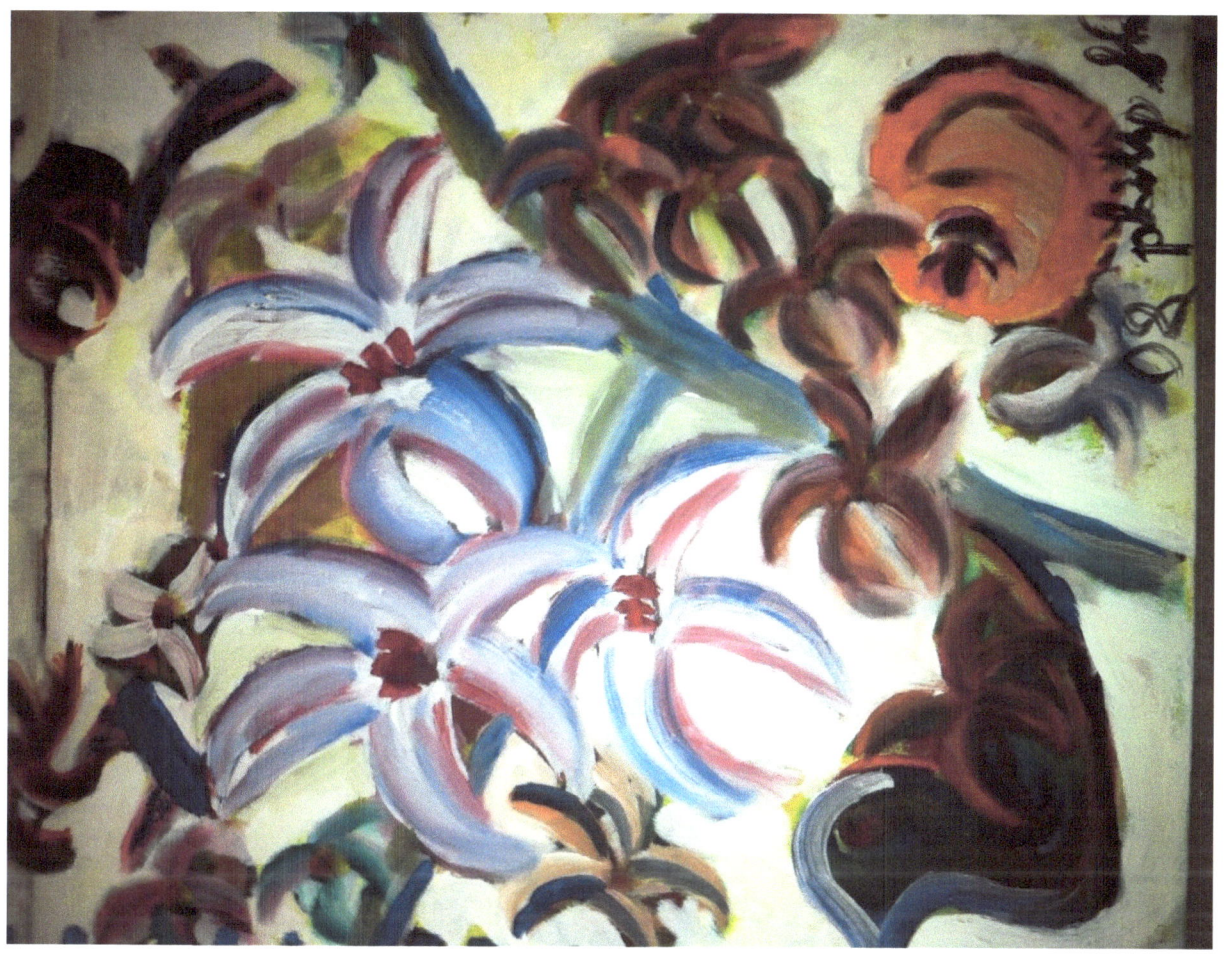

The sunflower becomes the white flower as I love you with the dirty mind as the poor white imagine face. You are more handsome than me as the white.

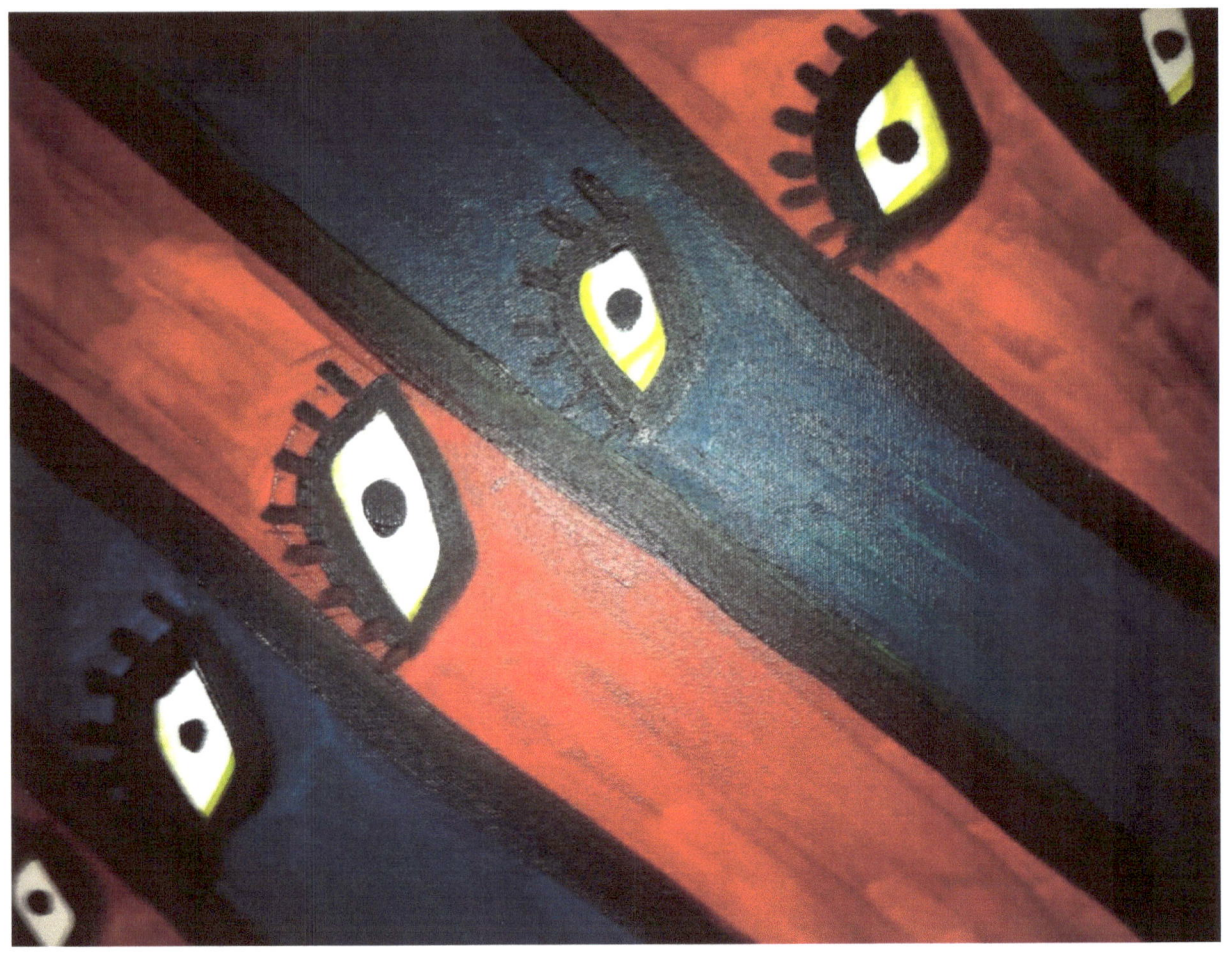

Under my feet, there was the monster eyes on it, I feel my mind pain as the scary touch of the imagine. A lot of eyes is opening and closing on my feet.

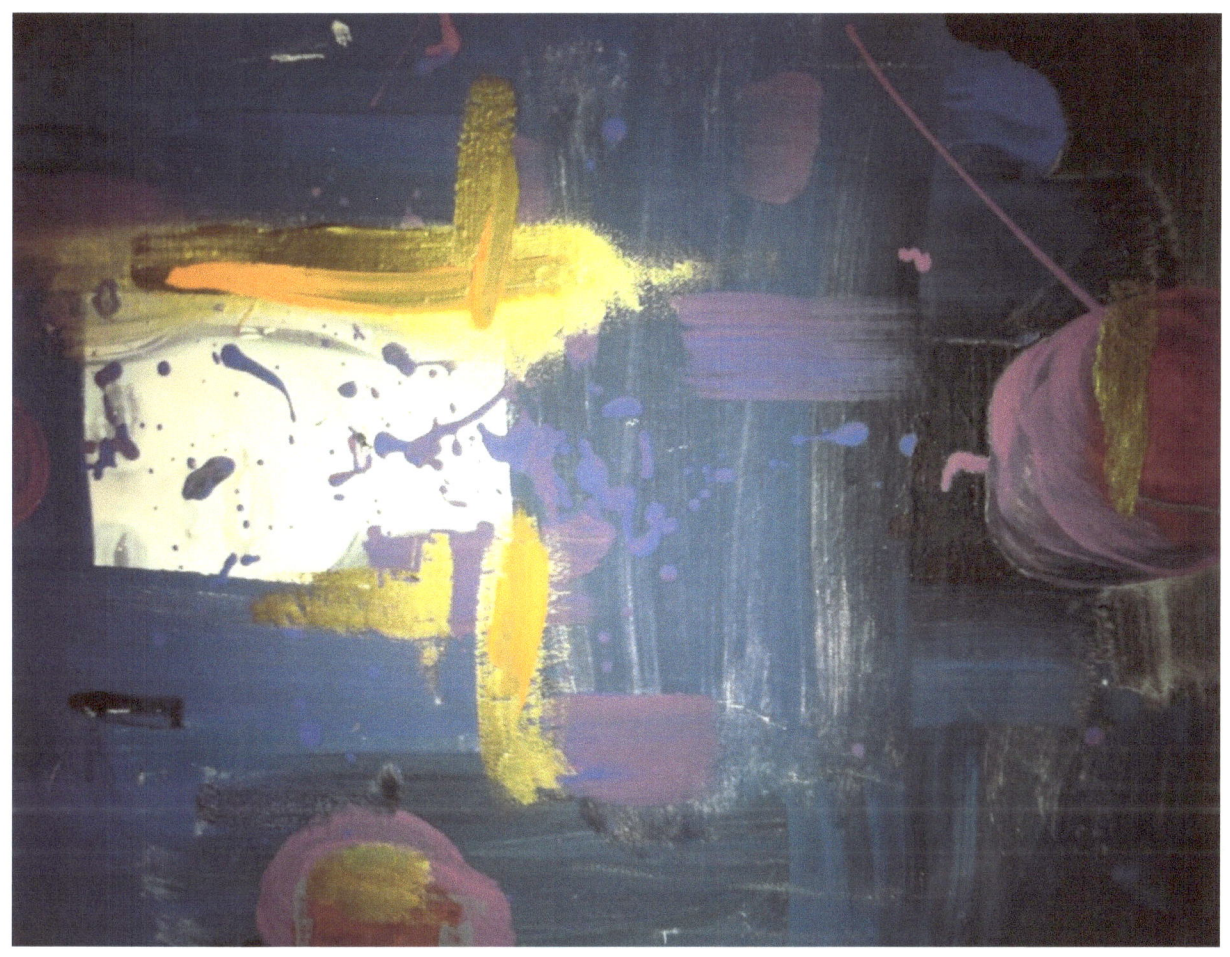

So I sleep tight on blue mood and I dream into the cross to be hang up on, until my lover is coming on to me.

She is maybe the movie actor.

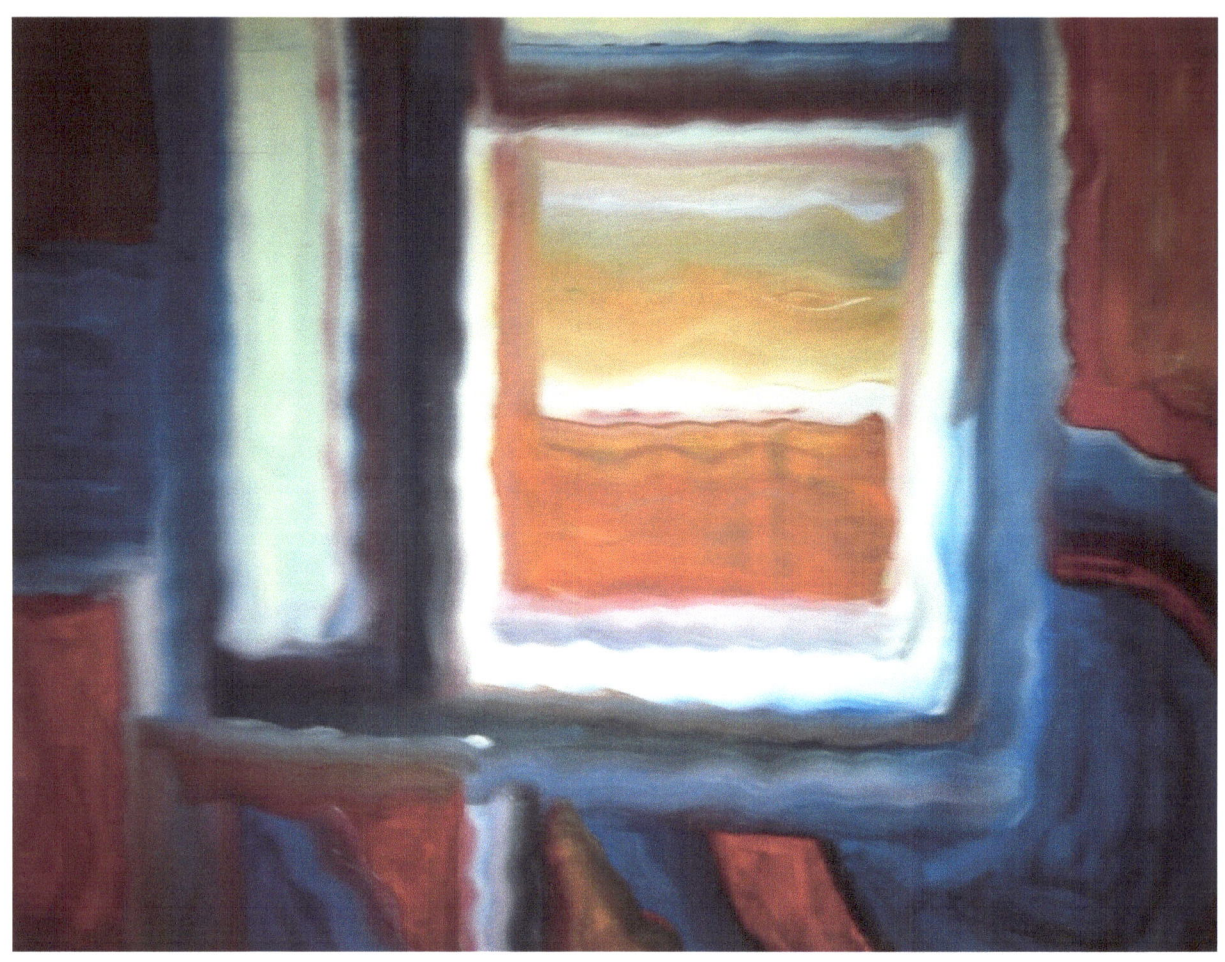

I feel dizzy and I love in the red blood mood to love you. It is comfortable but pain also I am melancholy. The two face of the love and pain at once in the square picture.

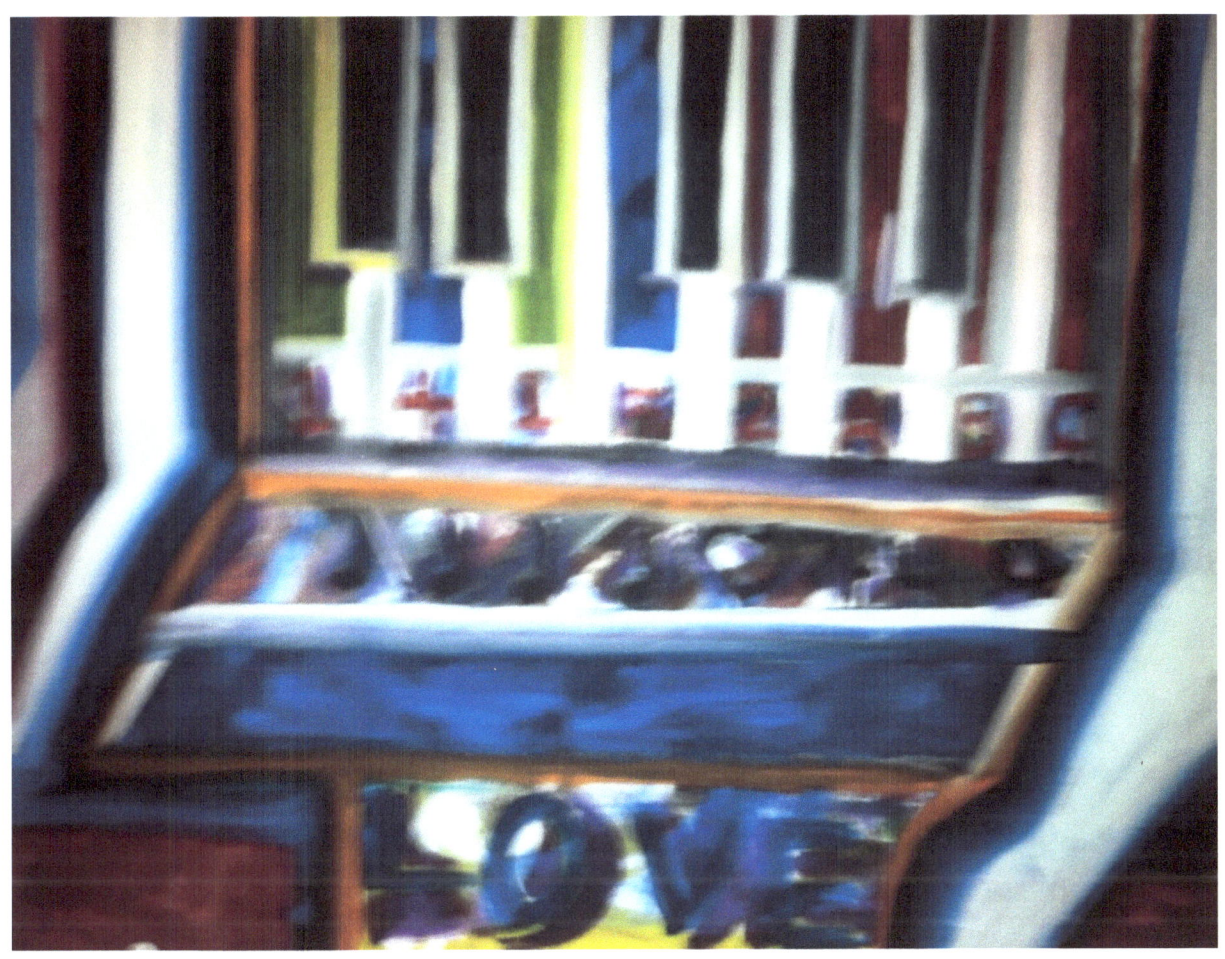

In my dream, I play the piano to play and I drumming my finger on your face to call you. Touching the rain like my finger drum.

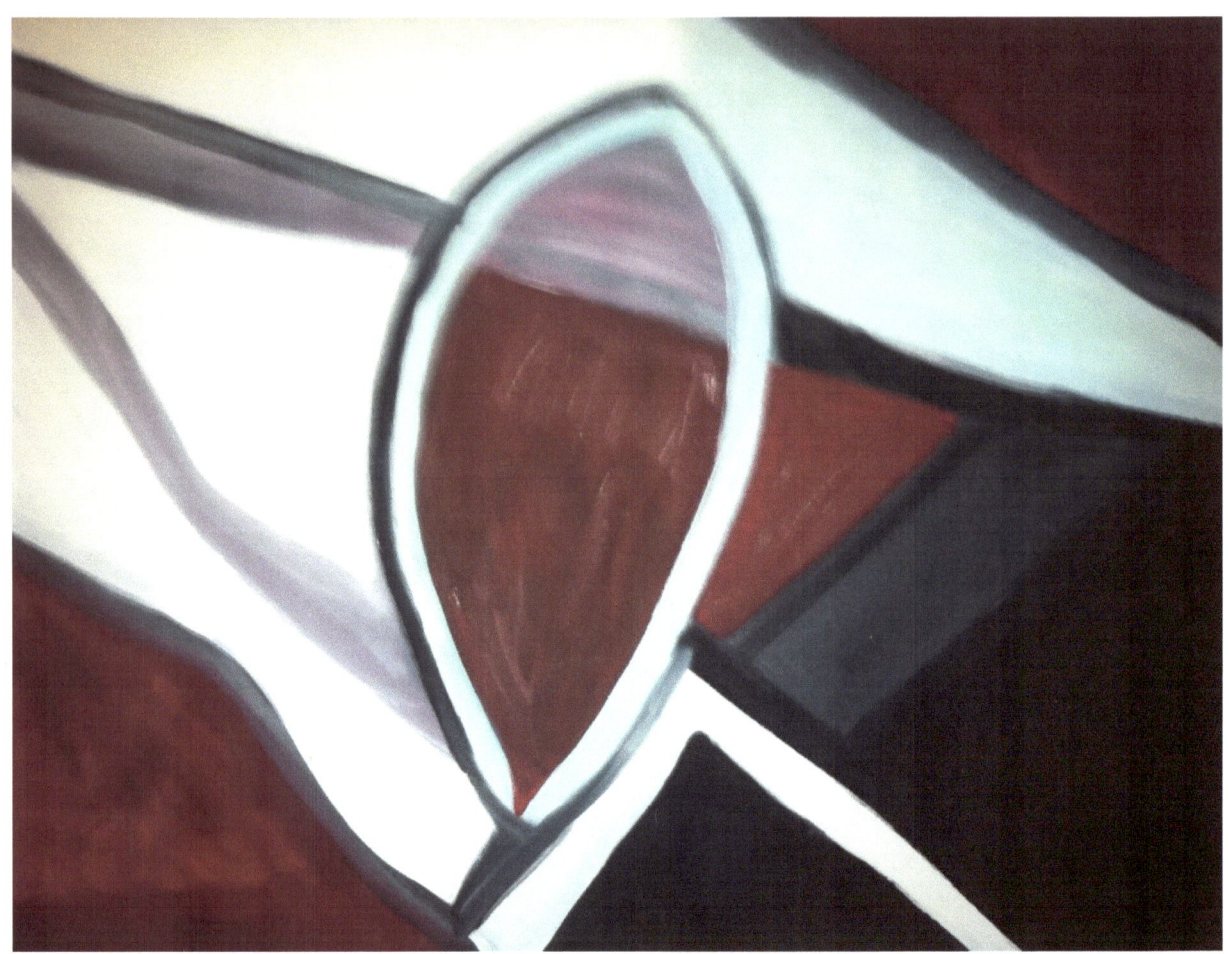

As the kiss, the line complex for the love as the circle. It is made up as the perfect structure for the art and painting to draw the cross.

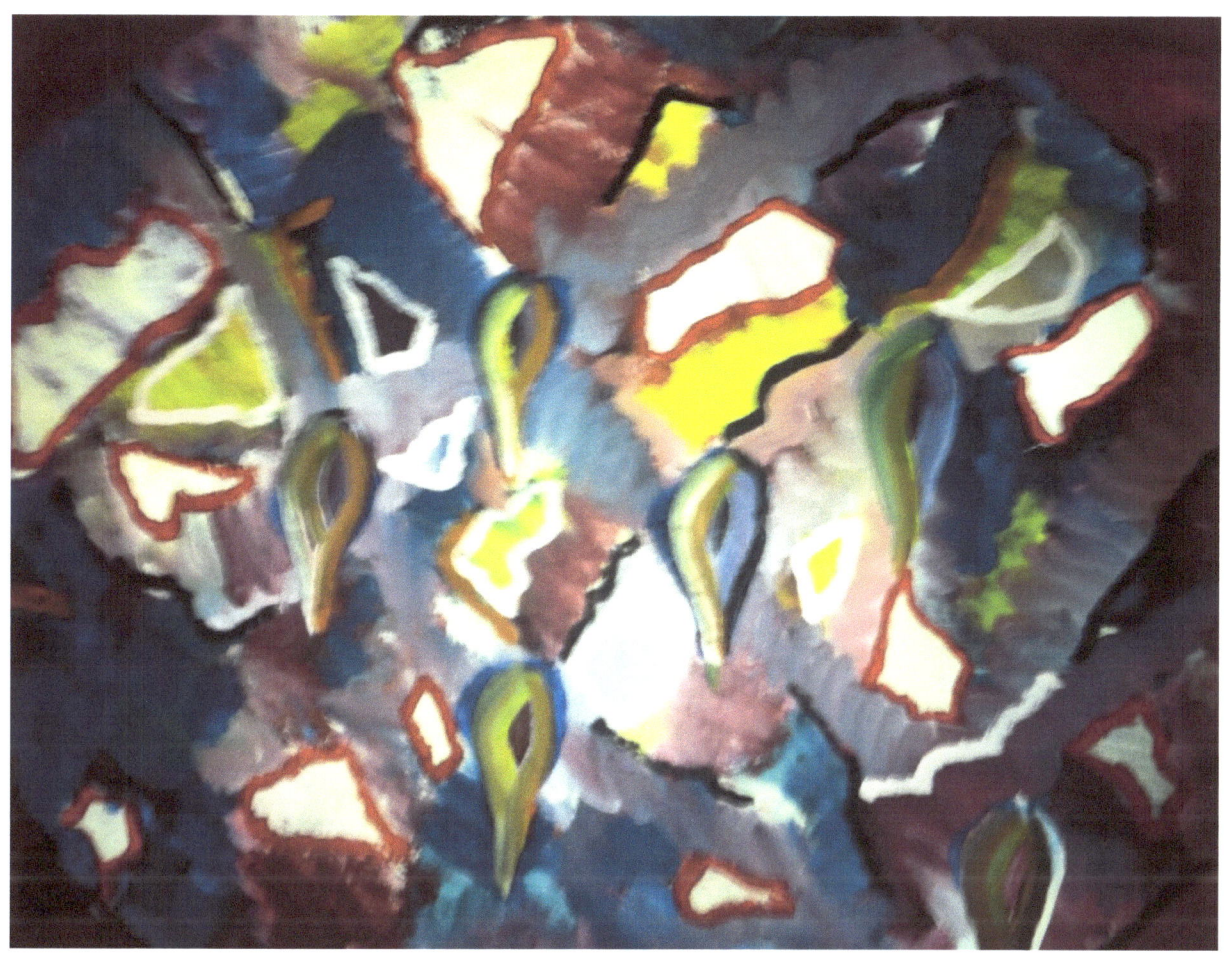

The raindrop on the cross when I was hang on there. It is my country way to draw the abstract picture, so I like it, too. As Jesus love his people.

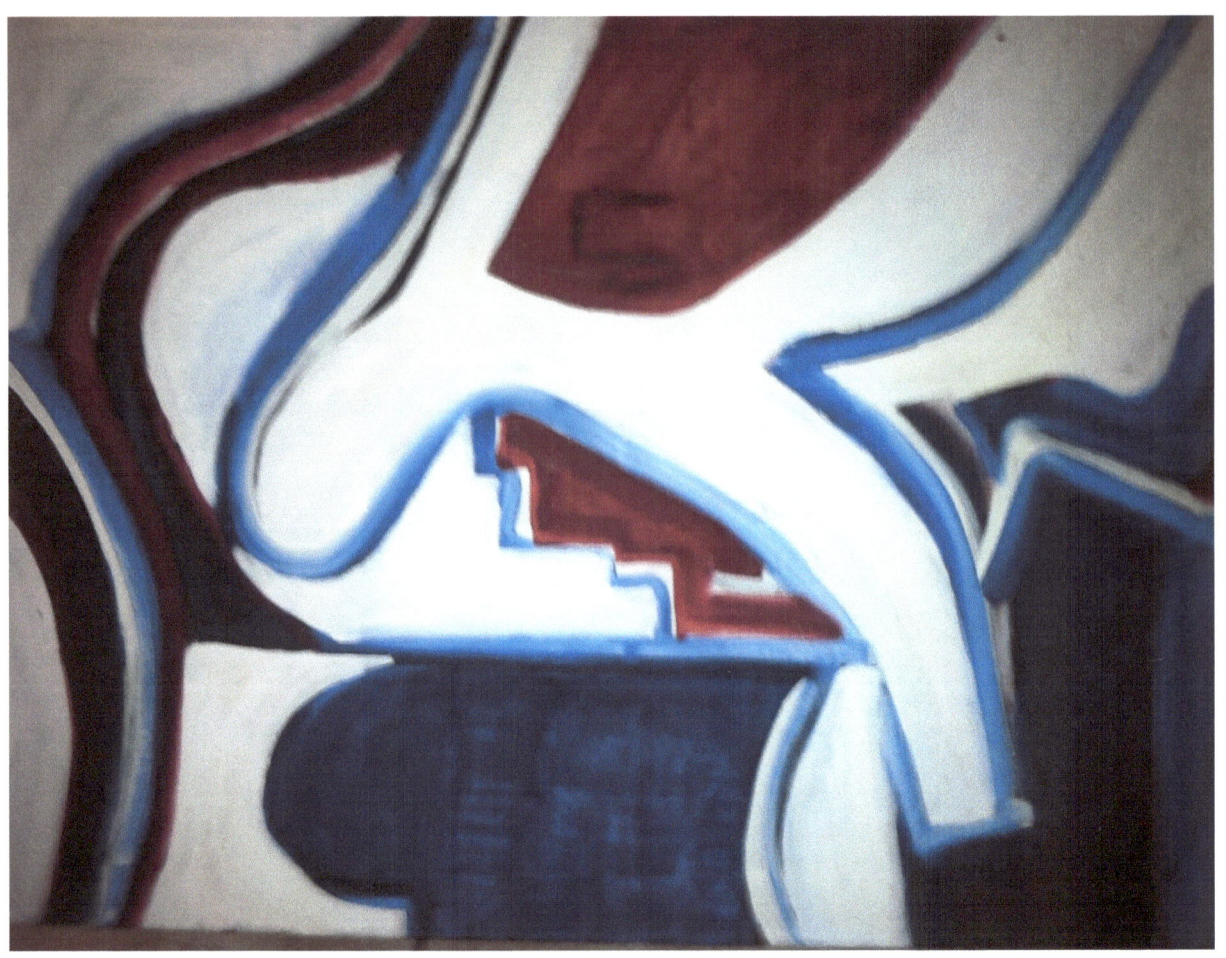

And I called you to my bed to love the woman. It is kind of ghost and the Madonna to call your soft face.

And I saw the sunglass woman in the seashore, and She is a fat but good looking with the black sun glass so she is living from the star and I love country where she is from.

Maybe the boy in my friend will jealous with me with clean twinkle eyes and the fancy boy. He is fancy as he is envy for my girl friend.

When the boy loves the sunglass girl, she gave her cute teeth to the boy as the psycho love selfishly. The devil has the cute teeth face.

And when she shows her eye to the boy, her cute demon face becomes the beautiful farm green face to love all of the people.

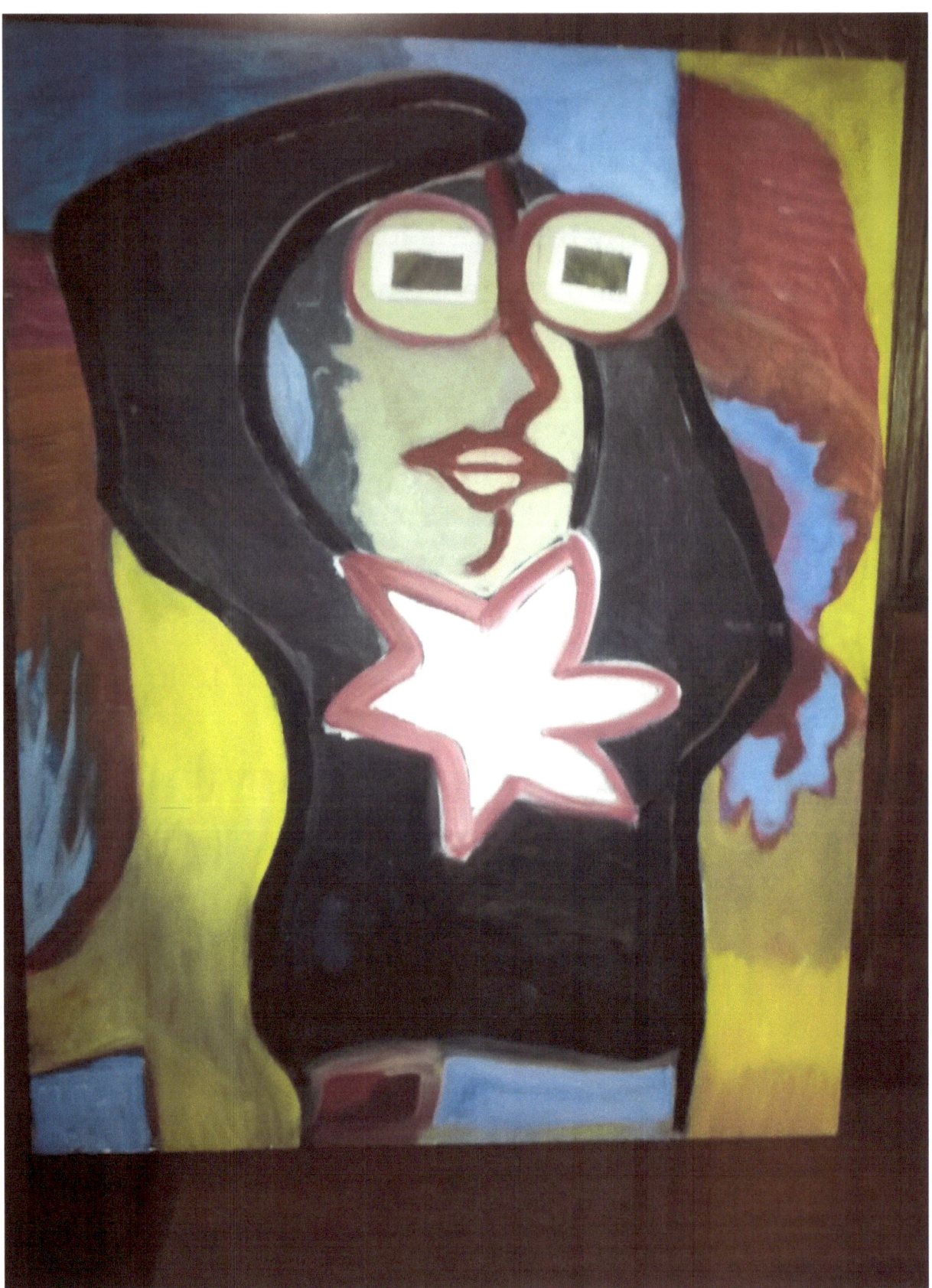

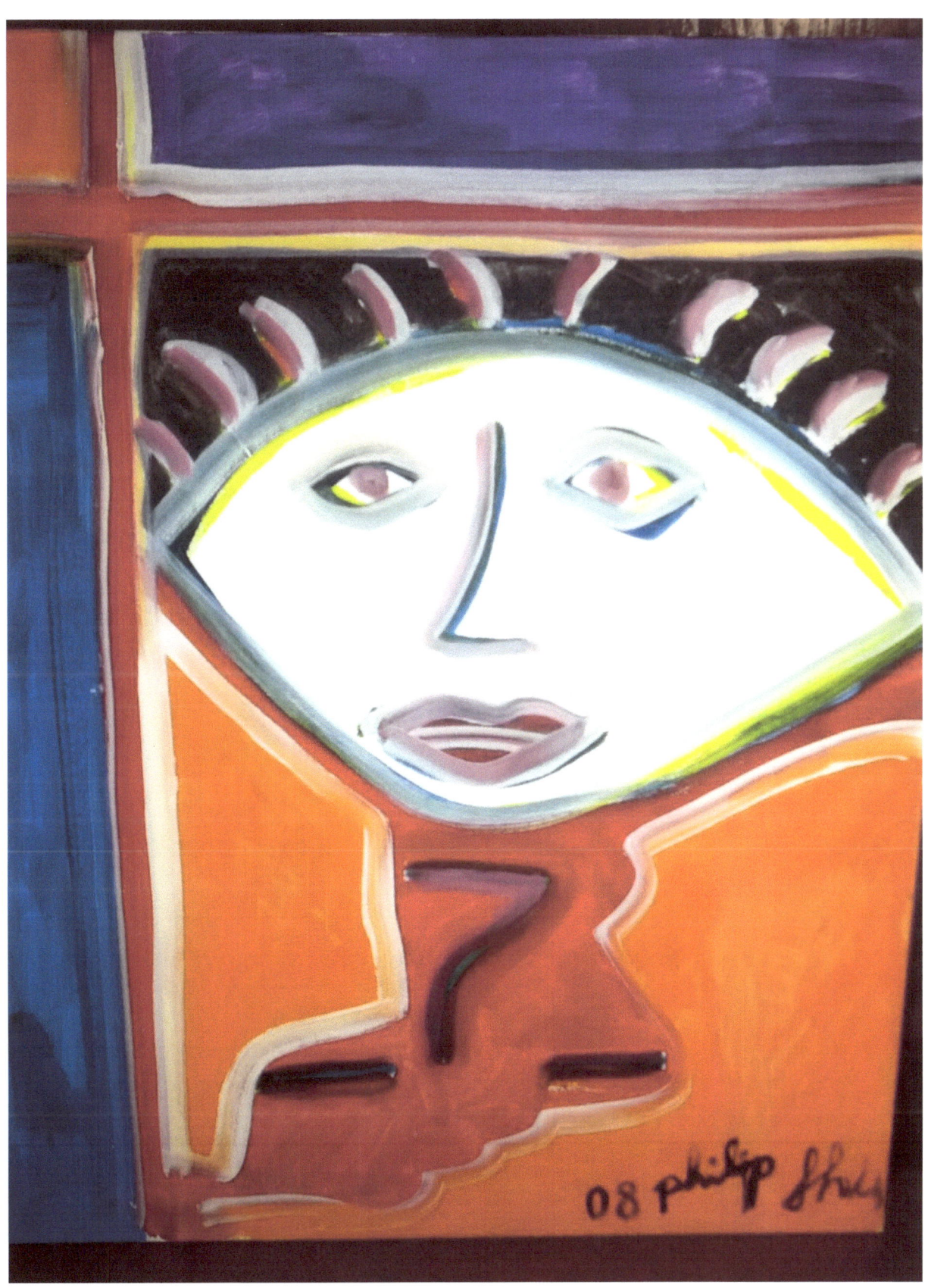

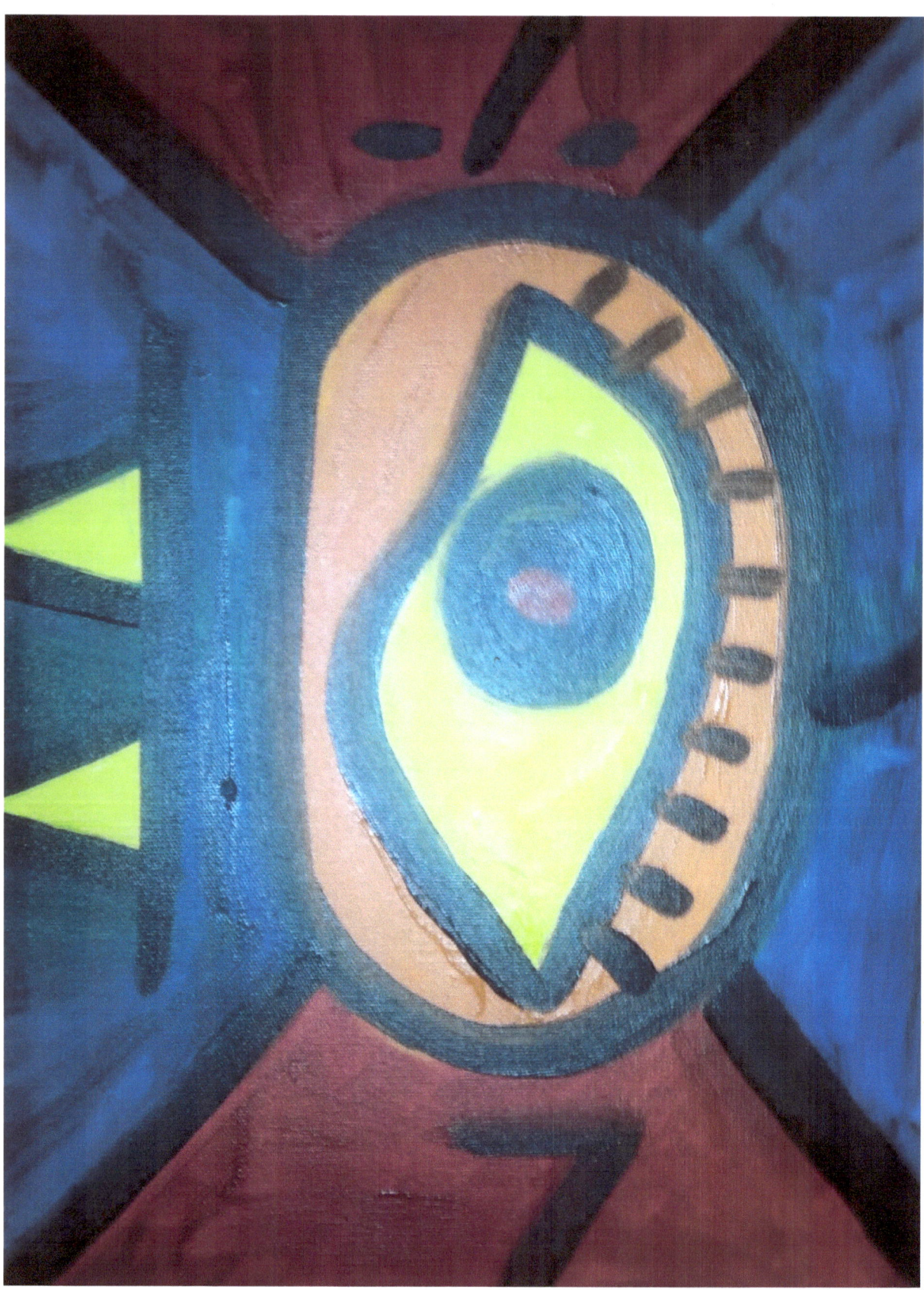

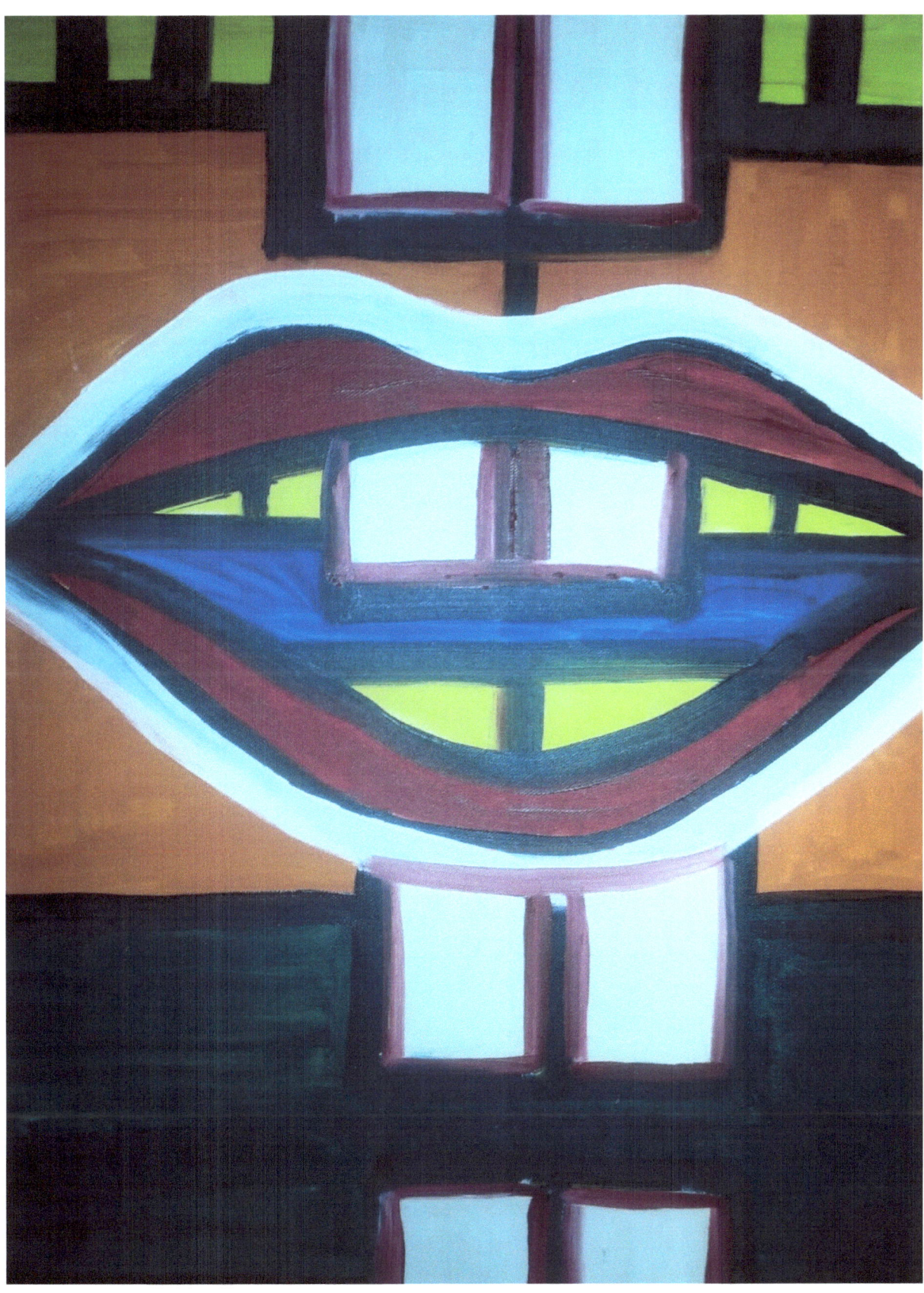

So I like to draw the flower as the flower is the best imagine and not reality to love it. The first flower is orange as the letter for the clean girl but here, it is shame to love the boy as the light.

And the girl is soft as the mature woman and not a girl anymore. She is lady in this middle green color.

But when I fly with the girl together, we really fly as the Jesus is savior and we will go to the heaven.

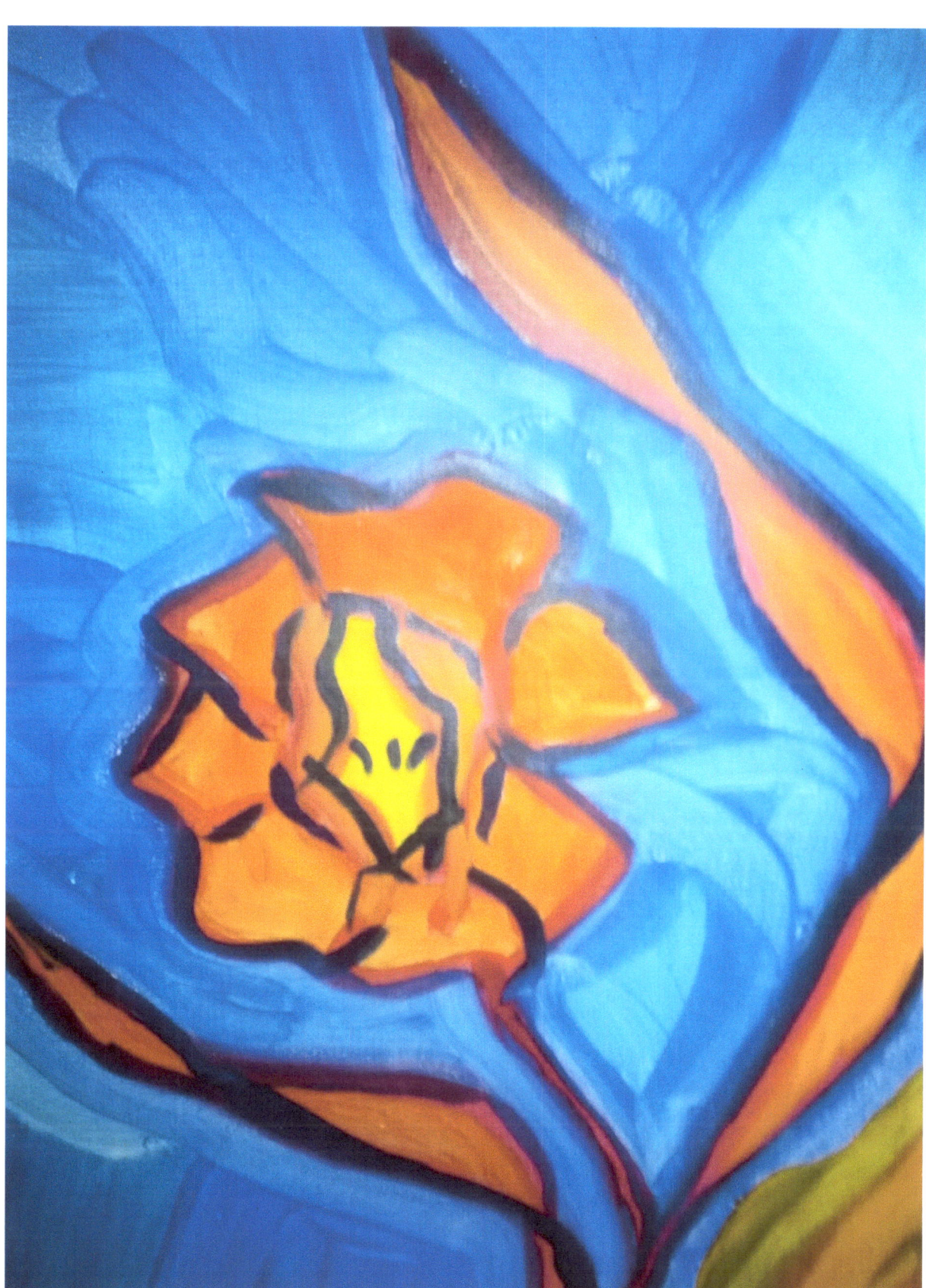

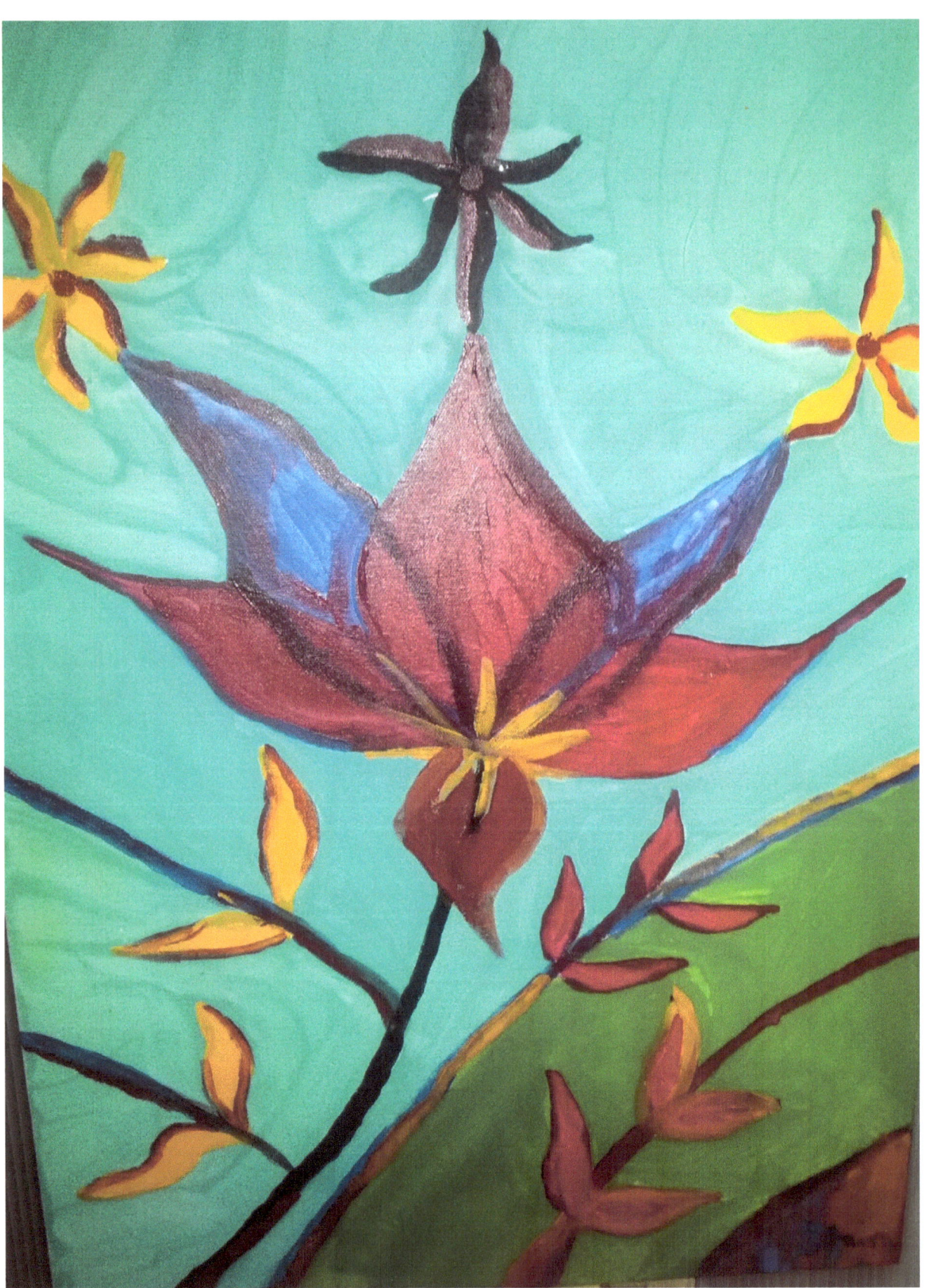

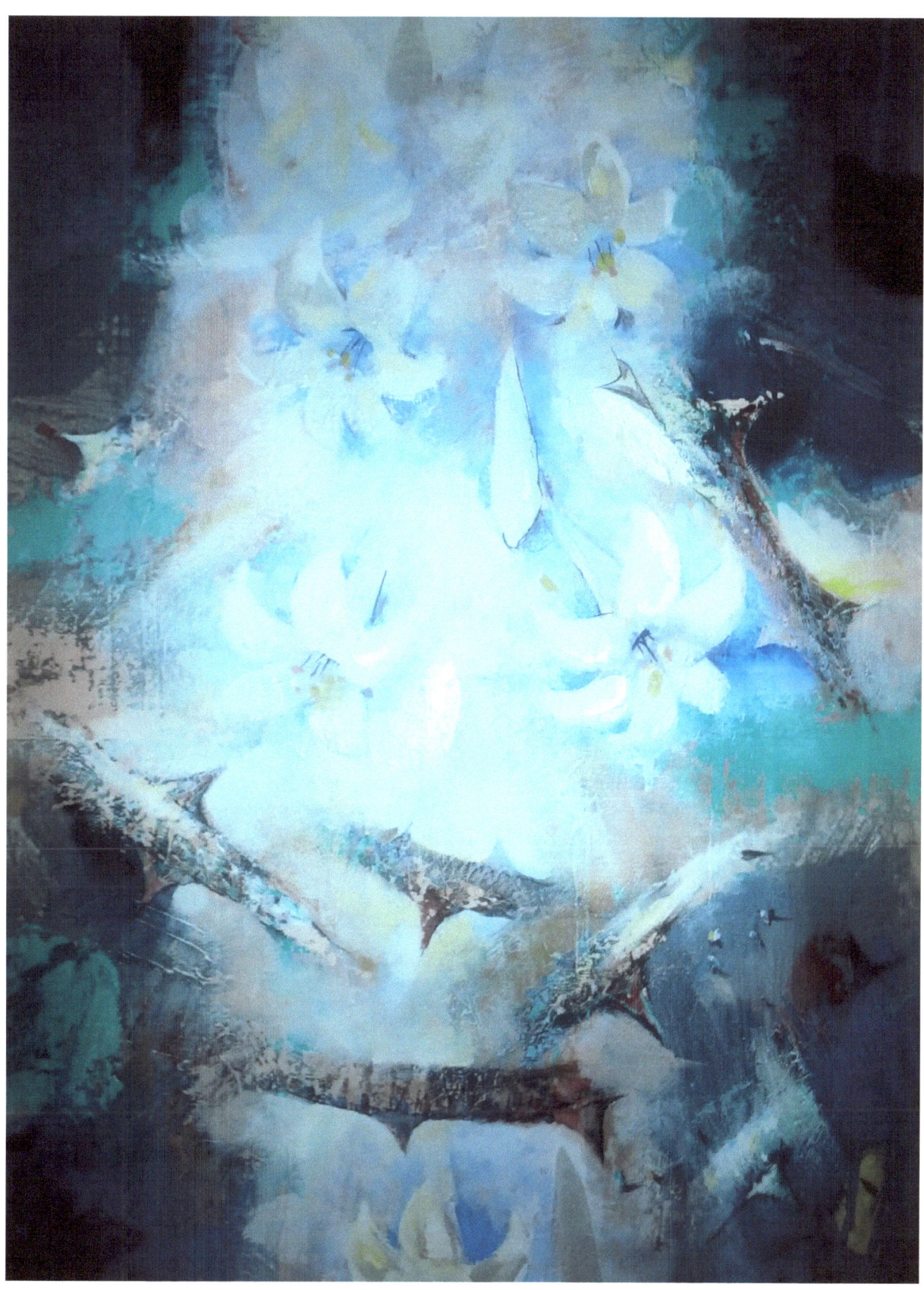

And after all, we are the artist to paint the picture to love in the sharp fancy and illusion. And I love this picture to draw in my life. The art is my dream life to live as I made the imagine picture.

www.ingramcontent.com/pod-product-compliance
Lightning Source LLC
Chambersburg PA
CBHW050404180526
45159CB00005B/2150